EMOTIONAL EXPRESSION
IN INFANCY

EMOTIONAL EXPRESSION IN INFANCY

A BIOBEHAVIORAL STUDY

ROBERT N. EMDE,
THEODORE J. GAENSBAUER,
and ROBERT J. HARMON

Psychological Issues
Monograph 37

INTERNATIONAL UNIVERSITIES PRESS, INC.

New York

Copyright © 1976, International Universities Press, Inc.

All rights reserved. No part of this book may be reproduced by any means, nor translated into a machine language, without the written permission of the publisher.

Library of Congress Cataloging in Publication Data
Emde, Robert N.
  Emotional expression in infancy.

  (Psychological issues ; vol. 10, no. 1 : Monograph ; 37)
  Bibliography: p.
  Includes Index.
  1. Infant psychology. 2. Emotions 3. Expression. I. Gaensbauer, Theodore J., joint author. II. Harmon, Robert John, 1946-   joint author. III. Title. IV. Series. [DNLM: 1. Child   development. 2. Child psychology. 3. Emotions—In infancy and childhood. W1 PS572 v. 10 no. 1 / WS105 E53e]
  BF723.I6E45   155.4'22   76-4609
  ISBN 0-8236-1651-7

Manufactured in the United States of America

To our families

CONTENTS

Part IV
WHERE ARE WE NOW?

ACKNOWLEDGMENTS

The story of how this monograph came about involves a number of people whose stimulation, encouragement, and hard work were pivotal. I would like to thank them all and acknowledge them individually by recounting a chronology.

The work had its origin in a separation. René Spitz left Denver in 1963 for Geneva. He left after having engaged me as a psychiatric resident in the research enterprise known in today's trade circles as "baby-watching." The research had been enormously pleasurable. How could it miss? Among other aspects, the experimental subjects were smiling babies. But there were also hours of pleasurable supervisory sessions which my colleague, Paul Polak, and I had with René, who opened our eyes so that we could look in a new way: naturalistically, patiently, systematically, and yet eager for surprise. When he left, I toyed with the idea of continuing to do research in infancy, but things did not seem the same. Further development was possible only after Herbert Gaskill gave vigorous encouragement to my designing a research program in the Department of Psychiatry at the University of Colorado School of Medicine. I searched for direction and found myself continually returning to a small book of Spitz's. For some reason, the book was not one which he had discussed with us and I soon discovered that, unlike his other works, it had not made a noticeable impact on the literature of child development or psychoanalysis. Yet its ideas kept playing in my mind. What crystallized then was a conviction that *A Genetic Field Theory* *of Ego Formation* (Spitz, 1959) raised important questions which could orient a research program.*

Two colleagues played a central role in the planning of this work and in its early phases of data collection. Although they remained as valued consultants throughout the project, they were afterwards prevented from a more intensive involvement because of other commitments. The initial formulations for the research were tested and reworked over several years with David Metcalf, whose enthusiasm, broad interdisciplinary knowledge, and hard-nosed interest in the developing central nervous system were invaluable. But he contributed even more. The research space used for the project was in large part developed by him and he has been an inspired teacher about the EEG and polygraphic techniques. In addition, he was the primary reader of EEGs during the year-long study. Kenneth Koenig entered the project during the planning and pilot phase of the year-long study. His sense of relevance, critical mind, energizing good will, and sense of humor kept the project going during uncertain early times of data collection. Without his expertise in photography, our project would not have been possible.

Herbert Gaskill did more than provide the impetus for the project. As department chairman and sponsor of my Research Scientist Development Award, he offered continual encouragement and guidance, as well as the freedom to explore and develop.

The initial longitudinal study was carried out primarily for another purpose, but it allowed for the testing of ideas and collection of some data presented here. The collaboration of Katherine Tennes, Anthony Kisley, and David Metcalf in that study is gratefully acknowledged.

The support of the Research Development Program, Na-

---

*René Spitz died on September 14, 1974 after spending a final five years in Denver. He had the pleasure of seeing many of his ideas generating research in this project and in others of the Developmental Psychobiology Research Group at the University of Colorado Medical School.

tional Institute of Mental Health (Award No. K2-36,808) has been, in every sense, what has allowed the work to progress through the nurturence of its Principal Investigator since 1967. The encouragement of Robert Wallerstein, Mary Haworth, and the "father" of the program, the late Bert Boothe, is especially appreciated. The support of the National Institute of Mental Health Project Grant Nos. MH 13803 and MH 15753 is also gratefully acknowledged.

My two coauthors joined the project during the early phase of data collection for the year-long longitudinal study. Since then we have developed and carried out the research enterprise together. We would like to give especial thanks to the two coordinating secretaries of our project. Jean Hearn Livingston served as receptionist, schedule coordinator, typist, and occasional experimenter in our social-interaction series for four years of the project. Margaret Purdum performed similar duties and also handled the entire typing, checking, and correspondence relating to this manuscript. Both women gave of their intelligence, efficiency, and personal charm for many long hours well beyond the call of duty. Finally, special thanks are due Joseph Campos, George Morgan, Douglas Ramsay, and John Merriweather, who gave generous amounts of their time and creative efforts to criticizing early versions of the manuscript.

Robert N. Emde
Denver, Colorado, 1974

PART I

THE WHY AND HOW OF THE STUDY

1

THEORETICAL BACKGROUND

There is little in life more quietly dramatic than a mother's moment of discovery that her baby is beaming at her with sparkling eyes. A week ago, or a month ago, he was less responsive, less human. Now, when he looks at her, he smiles, and they are seemingly joined in a new world of mutually pleasurable communications. Another moment, often perceived as dramatic but not quiet, occurs when her baby, now older, cries upon the approach of a stranger.

These developmental events, full of meaning for the baby's mother and family, are a central focus of this monograph. To be sure, we studied them because they have practical social importance, but we also chose to study them because they have broader theoretical interest. The dramatic onset of these infant behaviors seemed to indicate a discontinuity with previous development. It was as if they occurred suddenly and without obvious antecedents. But how could this be? Thinking about this question led to our program of study.

DISCONTINUITIES AND CONTINUITIES IN DEVELOPMENT

The question of discontinuities in development is not new. In the field of child development the issue of whether the developmental process is entirely continuous has been long debated. Is not development sometimes discontinuous, with abrupt changes resulting in new qualities? Until recently, an emphasis

3

on continuity has predominated, an emphasis bolstered by scientific advances which have come from experimental learning studies. But now, as is clear in recent data to be reviewed below, there is a resurgence of interest in the investigation of discontinuities.

The field of psychoanalysis has a history which differs from that of child development. As originally stated, its genetic psychology was a discontinuous one. Freud postulated that psychosexual development occurs as a series of qualitative changes: Oral, anal, and phallic stages each have emergent qualities, and are hierarchically subsumed and integrated during the subsequent reorganization which takes place during puberty (Freud, 1905). Freud later added a developmental anxiety series which also contains qualitative changes (1926), and still later Erikson added a psychosocial series with epigenetic stages occurring throughout the life span (1950). In the light of this background, it is curious that recent psychoanalytic literature often gives the impression that these stages are more a perspective than a historical reality, that they are tools for reconstruction as one views what is essentially a continuous stream of life.

An either/or quality often seems to pervade discussions about discontinuities in development, perhaps because the concept of "discontinuity" is often interpreted as meaning a total interruption. Obviously, total interruption does not occur. A concise statement of the discontinuity-continuity issue, one which argues for the validity of both, appears in a textbook by Ausubel and Sullivan (1970):

> . . . whether growth is quantitative and continuous or qualitative and discontinuous is partly a function of the rate at which it is taking place. When the rate of change is slow, development tends to occur within the framework of qualitative constancy. All forms are consolidated or modified slightly to meet new conditions, and new elements are incorporated without any necessity for fundamental reorganization. A state of relative equilibrium and stability prevails. But when the rate of change is more rapid, qualitative differentiation also tends to occur. Es-

tablished patterns must either be discarded or undergo radical revision. Together with recently introduced components, they are reorganized into a qualitatively different Gestalt which is discontinuous with the antecedent condition of the organism; and until consolidation occurs, a state of relative instability and disequilibrium exists. In other instances, however, because of the operation of cushioning mechanisms, qualitative interstage growth is accomplished gradually without abruptness [pp. 98-99].

THE GENETIC FIELD THEORY AS AN ORGANIZER FOR RESEARCH

A Genetic Field Theory of Ego Formation, published by René Spitz in 1959, directs our attention to infant discontinuities. It specifies behavioral indicators of times of qualitative shift and focuses on emotional expressions. Although stated in terms of psychoanalytic metapsychology, it is a multidisciplinary theory. It combines principles of Gestalt psychology, embryology, ethology, and psychoanalysis with inferences from human infant observational research. We found this theory to have explanatory applicability to a considerable number of diverse recent research findings. We also found that it could be stated simply enough to design a research program for testing its usefulness.

A. A RESTATEMENT OF THE THEORY

It is important to make explicit that the theory rests on an organismic assumption. This assumption, which has its origins in the holistic view of Gestalt psychology, has been extraordinarily useful in theoretical biology (Goldstein, 1939; von Bertalanffy, 1934, 1952, 1968a) and developmental psychology (Werner, 1948; Werner and Kaplan, 1963). According to this assumption, the whole has a determining influence on the functioning of its parts; a full appreciation of any part function must involve consideration of the entire context. Thus, in Spitz's theory, the development of infant smiling is of necessity a part of the development of the infant's capacity to appreciate, to attend to, and to remember aspects of his environment, of the development of learning responses, and of his level of brain maturation.

The organismic assumption also implies a teleology. This teleology is usually encompassed within the adaptive point of view of psychoanalytic metapsychology. It involves both a biological and an ontogenetic aspect. Biologically, the human infant is born with a set of species-specific capacities, which have been molded by long time spans in evolution, and which guarantee that he is preadapted to the "average expectable environment" (Hartmann, 1939). Furthermore, species-wide maturational factors exert a continuing influence throughout development, affecting its "rate, range and tempo" (Schur, 1966) as well as possibly influencing the emergence of new behaviors. Biological adaptation refers to the species. On the other hand, there is an ontogenetic adaptation which refers to the progressive fitting in of the individual with his particular biosocial context. In most psychoanalytic literature the term "adaptive" is used only in the latter sense. But the former sense is equally crucial, for it implies that the human organism has a tendency to maintain its integrity when challenged by the environment and a tendency to grow in certain prescribed directions; at any given time, the significance of any developmental function will be determined by this larger context as well.

The central proposition of Spitz's theory is that rates of development in infancy are uneven. There are certain periods when both behavioral and physiological development proceeds at an increased pace. These times of rapid change are reflected in the emergence of new levels of organization and are followed by periods of slower change when developmental gains are consolidated and further differentiation begins to take place. Development is not only a process of steady accumulation; from the observer's point of view, it can be seen to occur in jumps. The organismic assumption necessarily implies that any rapid changes in brain maturation are likely to be reflected in multiple sectors of the developing personality and vice versa. Antecedent-consequent relationships in any developmental sequence are a matter for research. This proposition is at variance with the learning theorist's view of development, according to which there is a gradual enrichment through learned responses (see, for example, Watson [1930], Hull [1952], and the more recent reviews of Bijou and Baer [1961, 1965] and R. White [1963]), and with the cognitive view of Piaget (1936) in which continuous development is also emphasized. It is entirely consonant, however, with the "organismic" perspective of Werner's developmental psychology and with the genetic propositions of psychoanalysis. Spitz emphasizes his reliance on the model presented in *Three Essays on the Theory of Sexuality,* where Freud (1905) set forth his psychosexual theory, which is epigenetic and holistic in its implications.

Another proposition of Spitz's theory has to do with the changing relationship of maturation and experience, even within the confines of the first postnatal year. Initially, maturation will have the greater share in determining observable changes; toward the end of the first year its influence, while still demonstrable, is less prominent.

According to a third proposition, affect behaviors can serve as useful indicators of the times of rapid change. Specifically, the emergence of social smiling at two or three months and of distress at the approach of a stranger at eight months signal accelerated changes, not only in social-affective development but also in cognitive development and brain maturation. Why did Spitz choose affect behaviors as indicators? This choice was probably rooted in his clinical and theoretical interest in the central role of object relations and early ego development (Spitz, 1957, 1965), although he emphasized that it was somewhat arbitrary. From our point of view it has provided a unique opportunity for observing and for generating correlational research in developmental psychophysiology.

A fourth proposition of the theory is broader in scope and

encompasses the first three. Each time of rapid change reflects a major developmental shift to a new level of organization. It follows that novel functions and structures emerge, an example of creativity in development. Spitz quotes the embryologist Waddington: "A new level of organization cannot be accounted for in terms of the properties of its elementary units as they behave in isolation, but is accounted for if we add to these certain other properties which the units only exhibit when in combination with one another" (Waddington, 1940, as quoted by Spitz, 1959, p. 62).

This idea is also central to the developmental psychology of Werner and his students, and has been formulated as the "orthogenetic principle": "Organisms are naturally directed towards a series of transformations — reflecting a tendency to move from a state of relative globality and undifferentiatedness towards states of increasing differentiation and hierarchic integration" (Werner and Kaplan, 1963, p. 7).

Spitz borrows a term from embryology to describe this creative aspect of postnatal development — namely, the "organizer." Needham (1931) described an embryological organizer as a "developmental pacemaker for a particular axis" and as a "center radiating its influence" (as quoted in Spitz, 1959). Although he alludes to shifting terminology and concepts in the recent embryological literature, Spitz adopts the "organizer" for his genetic field theory because it allows for a dynamic description of the new relational factor in development. Thus the emergence of the "smiling response" is the indicator of the first period of rapid change which Spitz refers to as the "first organizer of the psyche." The emergence of "eight-months anxiety" (distress on the approach of a stranger) indicates the period of rapid change referred to as the "second organizer of the psyche." The emergent affect behavior is not the organizer, it merely indicates it. The organizer itself is a construct describing the formal properties of the new level of functioning. It describes the "new relational factor in development," the new way, or in Spitz's terms, the "new *modus operandi*" (Spitz, 1961) or the new "algorithm" (Spitz, personal communication) according to which development now proceeds.

Although Spitz emphasized the new mode of functioning in terms of selected landmark changes in ego development (especially object relations and the organization of perception), it is clear that he meant it to encompass a broad area of the "genetic field." In a later paper, he illustrated the usefulness of this approach for understanding early psychophysiological adaptation, and formulated a theory of infant physiological prototypes of later psychological defenses (Spitz, 1961). Indeed, recent scholarly works which put forth the idea of early psychophysiological modes as a bridge concept for (1) psychosomatic relationships (Spitz, 1961), (2) psychosocial functioning (Erikson, 1950), and (3) the integration of trace and schema memory theories (Wolff, 1967) all seem to indicate that this is an important idea whose time has come.

B. COMMENT AND CRITIQUE OF THE GENETIC FIELD THEORY

To those familiar with Spitz's theory it will be apparent that ours is an incomplete statement of it. Because this monograph is limited to our research on normal infants in their first postnatal year, we have not touched upon those aspects of the theory which deal with dependent development and critical periods, pathological outcomes, or a third major rapid change that occurs during the second year. Furthermore, we have used a different language to summarize the theory, a language calculated to relate it to our operational research needs. In the course of our research we found it necessary to reduce abstract concepts to more concrete principles and to ignore subtleties in favor of simple alternative statements. We certainly cannot presume that our condensation has captured the richness of the theory; we can only hope it has not substantially violated its meaning. Spitz deliberately couched the theory within the framework of psychoanalytic metapsychology. This decision led to many speculative statements concerning the development of the infant's subjective-experiential world. In summarizing the theory, our bias has been to lift it from its subjective-experiential referents insofar as possible and place it in an objective frame of reference for research analysis. We have selected, for example, the description of the smiling response as an indicator of a time of rapid global change in psychophysiological development rather than the description of it as an indicator "that the reality principle has been established" or that "the infant has acquired the capacity to rediscover in reality the object which corresponds to what is present in his imagination" (Spitz, 1959, p. 20).

Spitz's language in *A Genetic Field Theory* is a mixed one. Perhaps because of its position in crossing to new ground, the book contains not only descriptive behavioral concepts but also inferred experiential concepts; not only field concepts as described above, but also mechanistic concepts, such as tension reduction, energy displacement, and discharge. Mixed language, however, is not a problem unique to this theory. It pervades much of contemporary psychoanalytic literature, as has been discussed in a number of scholarly papers (e.g., Grossman and Simon, 1969; Klein, 1969; also Loewald, 1960, 1970; Peterfreund, 1971; and Holt, 1967). The history of early psychoanalytic theorizing includes the context of Freud's experience with the reflex model in neurology (Amacher, 1965; Holt, 1965) and the nineteenth-century *Zeitgeist* of *Naturwissenschaft* (Bernfeld, 1944). As Freud's clinical experience increased, his theorizing became less mechanistic and more concerned with meaning, conflict, and structure. Subsequent developments of the adaptational point of view (Hartmann, 1939) and ego psychology (A. Freud, 1936; Rapaport, 1959) have continued this line because of its usefulness in explaining data from the psychoanalytic setting. Outside of psychoanalysis, the necessity for a nonmechanistic view of human development is argued most forcefully by von Bertalanffy (1967). It also receives support from developments in neurophysiology and information theory (see Miller, Galanter, and Pribram, 1960).

Recent Findings in Developmental Psychology

A Genetic Field Theory was delivered as a lecture in 1958 and published in 1959. Since that time there has been an unprecedented growth in the "infant literature" of developmental psychology. In the second edition of Carmichael's *Manual of Child Psychology* (Pratt, 1954) the review of the literature on the very young child listed about 500 references. The corresponding chapter in the third edition (Kessen, Haith, and Salapatek, 1970), only 16 years later, contains four times that number of references. Recently, concentrated work has been devoted to affect behaviors and the development of sleeping and waking states. For the most part, studies have been experimental and cross-sectional; longitudinal studies emphasizing careful naturalistic description have been rare. Presumably because of the ready availability of hospitalized nursery infants, there has been an enormous overrepresentation of neonatal studies compared to studies of later infancy.

As one might surmise, the accumulation of data since *A Genetic Field Theory* was written is enormous. Although this theory is virtually unknown in developmental psychology,[1] many of the data which have been collected strongly support the existence of a discontinuity between the very young infant and the infant of two months and after. The period of later discontinuity postulated in *A Genetic Field Theory* to be around eight postnatal months is as yet neither supported nor controverted. Let us review some of this literature.

A. EVIDENCE FOR AN EARLY DISCONTINUITY

Surprisingly enough, the major body of research which has generated data inconsistent with the simple continuity interpretation comes from learning studies. That this could occur in a field whose originators were so openly motivated to

[1] *A Genetic Field Theory* is not cited in the most recent edition of *Carmichael's Manual of Child Psychology* (Mussen, 1970) nor is it referenced in a sampling of current textbooks on child development (e.g., McCandless, 1967; Stone and Church, 1975; Mussen, Conger, and Kagan, 1974; Bijou and Baer, 1965).

demonstrate developmental continuities (Watson, 1930) is a tribute to the careful methodology and respect for rules of evidence which has characterized recent work. Those who conducted studies in the early part of the century were enthusiastic in their demonstrations of learning in young children, both in Russia (see Razran, 1933, for a review) and in the United States (Watson and Watson, 1921; Jones, 1926). In 1931, Marquis wrote an article for the *Journal of Genetic Psychology* entitled "Can Conditioned Responses Be Established in the Newborn Infant?," and on the basis of her studies answered in the affirmative. But the most prodigious phase of research in infant conditioning has occurred over the past one and one-half decades, since Brackbill (1958) demonstrated the operant control of smiling at four months and Rheingold, Gewirtz, and Ross (1959) did the same for infant vocalizations at the same age. In 1967, Lipsitt, reviewing the growing number of experimental studies of infant learning, raised important methodological issues concerning controls in earlier studies. He concluded that it seemed difficult to demonstrate classical aversive conditioning in the first three weeks, although the modification of appetitional responses, such as sucking, seemed more promising. Soviet research with classical conditioning was producing similar findings; in 1962 Kasatkin was quoted as summarizing the situation as follows: ". . . with a few exceptions, conditioned reflexes are weak and unstable up till the 4th to 5th weeks of life. . . . A firm and well-expressed conditioned reflex is sometimes formed in the 4th week and almost always in the second month" (quoted in Brackbill, 1962, and Kessen, Haith, and Salapatek, 1970, p. 324). In a later review Kasatkin (1969) stated that, with auditory conditioning, stable conditioned responses do not occur before 32 days of age.

Operant conditioning of newborn sucking, on the other hand, has been achieved by Lipsitt and Kaye (1965), Kron et al. (1967), and Sameroff (1971), but learned modifications were short-lived.

Probably the most enlightening studies of learning in infancy have come from Papousek (e.g., 1961, 1967; Papousek and Bernstein, 1969). Using the infant's head-turning response in an experimental design which has aspects of both classical and operant conditioning, he has been able to study the rate of conditionability from birth through six months of age. Most of his studies were carried out in a research unit in Prague where infants lived with their mothers or trained surrogate mothers; subsequent findings came from a residential nursery in the United States. His findings are quite clear: conditioning in these circumstances is quite difficult to attain during the first month of life; there is a marked increase in conditionability during the second and third months of life. He emphasizes that individual differences are great but that the general validity of the findings is indicated by equivalent results obtained with a conditioned eyeblink technique.

On the basis of his review of the literature, and his own precisely controlled studies, Sameroff (1971) wrote an article whose title is a rerun of the 1931 Marquis title: "Can Conditioned Responses Be Established in the Newborn Infant: 1971?" He concluded that classical conditioning is difficult, if not impossible, to demonstrate before three weeks of age. Using Piagetian concepts, he reasoned that there must be a differentiation of response systems during these early weeks; it is only after this neonatal phase that these systems can be coordinated with other sensorimotor schemes, such as sucking or head turning. He also speculated that maturational factors may play a role in the transition between neonatal and postneonatal stages of learning. Indeed, as one reviews recent work on learning in infancy, one cannot help getting the impression that we are on the threshold of major discoveries concerning the changing parameters of learning during this period of life.

A similar group of age-related findings has emerged in the newer field of habituation research. Habituation refers to a response decrement which occurs under experimental conditions when a stimulus is repeatedly presented. It is distinguished from other types of response decrement (such as fatigue of receptor or response apparatus) by the demonstration that the response returns when a new stimulus is introduced which is similar to, but in some ways different from, the original stimulus. In their excellent review of this subject, Jeffrey and Cohen (1971) document the general failure to obtain clear evidence for habituation in infants under two months of age in a number of studies which have used visual and auditory stimuli. Beyond two months, however, habituation has been demonstrated in a variety of modalities and with a number of responses. The authors point out that this shift represents a major developmental change in the phenomena under investigation but so far not enough is known for us to understand underlying mechanisms. It is unknown, for example, to what extent the developmental changes represent primary changes in *perceptual organization* or *response organization*. Furthermore, habituation, like classical and operant conditioning forms of behavior modification, must involve mechanisms for *retention,* and our knowledge about the development of this capacity in early infancy is seriously deficient.

An age-related change in a major autonomic response system has been extensively studied by Graham and her associates (Graham and Clifton, 1966; Graham and Jackson, 1970; Jackson, Kantowitz, and Graham, 1971). Again there is a shift between the newborn period and the period from six to eight weeks and after. Characteristically, a tone presented to an older infant evokes a deceleration in heart rate, whereas before six weeks the response is typically one of acceleration. These investigators gave strong consideration to the role of maturation of higher nervous centers in this developmental shift but also pointed to the need for more research using low to moderately intense stimuli and other sensory modalities. This need was answered by subsequent studies which have found newborn cardiac deceleration under such conditions.

Kearsley (1973) obtained these results with auditory stimuli, Lipsitt and Jacklin (1971) with olfactory stimuli, Sameroff, Cashmore, and Dykes (1973) with a patterned visual checkerboard stimulus, and Pomerleau-Malcuit and Clifton (1973) with vestibular and tactile stimuli. There is a shift, but it is not an either/or phenomenon.

Research on the early development of sensation and perception has been extremely active since *A Genetic Field Theory* was written, and yet generalizations about rates of development, for the most part, cannot be drawn from it. Most of the research has been concerned with the range of perceptual abilities in the newborn. There are few studies beyond this time, outside of the visual modality. However, even with vision not enough is yet known about the breadth of changes to warrant conclusions about global changes in organization. There are, for example, indications that the period from two to three months is an important one for the development of visual accommodation (Haynes, White, and Held, 1965), depth perception (Fantz, 1961; Polak, Emde, and Spitz, 1964b), and for the development of preferences for complex and novel visual patterns (Brennan, Ames, and Moore, 1966; Fantz, 1964; Wetherford and Cohen, 1973). That there also may be shifts in visual scanning patterns is indicated by other recent work (Haith, 1973; Bond, 1972).

The work of Haith and his colleagues (Bergman, Haith, and Mann, 1971; Haith, 1969, 1975) on the early development of visual scanning is especially instructive. These investigators have devised an infrared video technique for recording a young infant's eye movements and the direction of looking in both light and dark conditions. In the newborn, endogenous patterns of "searching" eye movements are modulated by the crossing of lines or bars. A shift occurs at seven weeks of age when significant scanning of the face has its onset; at this age, there begins to be a prominent scanning of the region around the eyes (Bergman, Haith, and Mann, 1971). Such a finding corresponds to the naturalistic observations of the age of onset of eye-to-eye contact between mother and infant made by Robson (1967). As the reviews of Bond (1972) and Haith (1975) point out, preferential looking at faces before seven weeks is probably explainable in terms of its being a rich source of complexity.

However, since so many parameters of perceptual development remain unexplored, it could be that an equal number of responses are developing at other times. In addition, there is a crying need for longitudinal research on the rates of development of individual parameters. Kessen, Haith, and Salapatek (1970) conclude their recent review of this area as follows:

> The assortment of studies reported . . . is at once exciting and distressing. It has been clearly and repeatedly established that the normal newborn infant responds to stimulation in all sensory modalities; he is, in every sense, competent. Yet, demonstrations *that* the baby responds cannot substitute for careful studies of *how* response changes with variations in the dimensions of stimuli employed. . . . there are few studies of changes in sensitivity between the first few days of life and the time of rich and demanding differentiation made by the child near the end of the first year of life [p. 322].

Examination of early changes in affect organization is a central aspect of the work to be presented in this monograph. Much of the recent literature which is relevant to our specific studies will be reviewed later. At this point it is important to note that in *A Genetic Field Theory,* Spitz sketched an outline of the phenomenology of affective development which has held up rather well. In the first two postnatal months, the one major affect expression is crying. When the infant's needs are met, he stops crying and becomes quiet, often returning to sleep. The onset of the social smile after this time signals a rather abrupt change, not only in the infant-mother relationship but in the psychophysiological development of the infant's affect organization; Spitz speculates that pleasure is now possible.

Several studies have systematically charted the onset and course of the social smile in a variety of settings (Ambrose,

1961; Polak, Emde, and Spitz, 1964a; Gewirtz, 1965). The onset of the predictable social smile does occur around two months. It does seem to "burst forth upon the scene," although it has precursors in irregular and nonspecific smiling, as our work will show. Wolff's (1959, 1963) careful naturalistic descriptions of early smiling and crying form an important background for our work.

B. EVIDENCE FOR A LATER DISCONTINUITY

Research on learning and perceptual development after three months, and particularly during the latter half of the first year, is so limited that any statements about times of rapid change are unwarranted. Literature relevant to the development of affect expressions will be summarized in subsequent chapters.

NEURAL BASES FOR BEHAVIORAL DISCONTINUITY IN EARLY INFANCY

The notion of behavioral discontinuity becomes much less mysterious when we look at how the brain develops. From every view, whether neurological, neurophysiological, or neuroanatomical, an overriding principle emerges: in early infancy growth is less by steady accretion and more by irregular jumps. Our attention is continually drawn to changes in quality rather than to changes in quantity.

A. EVIDENCE IN THE HUMAN

Pediatric neurology has enumerated a host of reflexes which are most active within the first two months and decline thereafter. Among these are the Babkin reflex, the steppage reflex, the palmar grasp, the Moro, and the tonic neck reflex. Because they decline and do not normally reappear after early infancy, they are often referred to as "transitory reflexes" of the newborn and their decline is thought to reflect the postnatal maturation of forebrain inhibitory areas (see reviews in Peiper, 1963; Paine, 1965; Parmelee and Michaelis, 1971).

On the tissue level of anatomy, Conel's classic works (1941, 1947) document the changes which occur in the human cerebral cortex during the first postnatal months; however, a precise knowledge of rates of change is lacking. The same could be said for other early rapid postnatal changes which have been documented, changes in (1) dendritic arborization, (2) increased vascularization of the brain, (3) myelinization, (4) glial proliferation, and (5) postnatal neurogenesis in limited areas (Altman, 1967; Bekoff and Fox, 1972). In their recent review of postnatal neural ontogeny, Bekoff and Fox (1972) concluded that myelinization in the human infant does not occur uniformly but in pulses or waves; furthermore, one system of fibers may start this process and then slow down and be surpassed by another system in which the process began later. They illustrate this by reference to the auditory and visual systems. The acoustic pathway is myelinated to the level of the inferior colliculus by eight fetal months, whereas the optic fibers do not undergo myelinization until after birth. In spite of this, optic projection fibers to the cortex become myelinated ahead of tracks from the cochlear nuclei.

B. A POSSIBLE ANIMAL MODEL

In a recent paper, Parmelee, Stern, and Harris (1972) have invoked a compelling, albeit speculative, explanation for a discontinuity which can be seen in the early development of human respiration. In the younger premature infant (less than 30 weeks postconceptual age) the pattern of respiration is more or less regular; periodic pauses or apneic episodes are relatively infrequent. Then, as he ages, he passes through a time when periodic respirations are characteristic of a signifi-cant amount of the time he is sleeping. It is only later, after the full-term age of 40 postconceptual weeks is reached, that the periodic pattern diminishes. It then gives way to regular respirations, thereafter the characteristic pattern of quiet sleep. The problem, then, is how to explain a neurophysiological control system which regulates a respiratory pattern and which goes from regular to periodic to regular again in developmental sequence.

Parmelee relies on the study of Hoff and Breckenridge (1954), in which the respirations in normal adult cats were compared with those of cats who were transected at pontine and medullary levels of the brain stem. They found that the medullary cat had a nonperiodic respiratory pattern, the pontine cat had a periodic pattern, and the intact animal had a nonperiodic pattern. They concluded:

> When the respiratory system is at its lowest level of integration . . . breathing is non-periodic. This is because the fundamental, primitive sub-stratum of breathing is non-periodic. When the respiratory system is fully integrated . . . breathing is also non-periodic. . . . at all levels in between, integration is incomplete, and the intrinsic slow rhythm is more facilitated than suppressed and finds expression in periodic breathing of one kind or another [p. 41].

Parmelee points out that in the premature a given segment is not completely organized before it interacts with the next higher level of control in the hierarchy, as is true in the adult cat transection experiments. However, it seems plausible to propose, as does Parmelee, that an analogous series of mechanisms comes into play in human ontogenesis as progressive forebrain encephalization occurs.

The reader may be jolted at the conjuring up of a cat in proposed explanations of human infant discontinuities. After all, in experimental animal research we know that the species *felix domestica* is even more overrepresented than is the nursery newborn in infant observational research. The cat is not only readily available, it is also generally cooperative and sleeps most of the time. Nevertheless, there is much to support the use of the kitten as an experimental animal model for our understanding of early sleep-wakefulness development in the human. Not unexpectedly, its postnatal development is more rapid than the human's but similar events occur. As in the human infant, the amount of the active form of sleep diminishes with development as wakefulness and drowsiness increase (Chase and Sterman, 1967). Also corresponding to human ontogenesis, the quiet form of sleep increases and becomes predominant (McGinty, 1971). Also in analogy to the human newborn, the very young kitten often enters active sleep with eye movements from an alert state (Jouvet-Mounier, Astic, and Lacote, 1970).

It appears that a major organismic shift occurs in the early postnatal weeks of the kitten's development, and McGinty (1971) has mustered experimental evidence to correlate this finding with what he refers to as "the encephalization of the neural control of sleep." His proposition is that the newborn's sleep in general, and most of the active portion of sleep in the adult, is controlled by the brain stem. It is during postnatal development that these brain-stem mechanisms come progressively under the control of higher-level forebrain mechanisms, resulting in more quiet sleep, less active sleep, and other changes.

But most compelling for our interest in the neurophysiological bases of organismic discontinuities is the precise experimental work done on the maturation of two brain-stem reflexes in the kitten by Chase (1970, 1971, 1972, 1973). In a preparation in which the moving kitten could be continually monitored for EEG, eye movements, and EMG, and in which the reflexes in question could be stimulated and recorded with implanted electrodes, Chase found consistent results. With regard to the monosynaptic masseteric reflex (sensory-V and motor-V), the kitten before two weeks had the highest amplitude reflex response in active sleep, a lower response in quiet sleep, and the lowest response in wakefulness. This pattern is exactly the opposite of what is found in the adult cat, where reflex amplitude is highest in wakefulness and lowest in active sleep. But even more remarkable is the fact that the maturation to the adult state-related pattern, with its complete reversal of the earliest pattern, is completed by six postnatal weeks! The polysynaptic digastric reflex showed a similarly dramatic pattern, with the under-two-weeks animal showing highest reflex amplitude in active sleep, less in quiet sleep, and least in wakefulness, as was true for the masseteric reflex. The shift of this reflex to the adult pattern took place even more rapidly and also involved a developmental reversal, the amplitude of the reflex being smallest during active sleep instead of largest. However, unlike the masseteric reflex, in the adult pattern quiet sleep did not maintain an intermediate position but became the state during which amplitude was highest. Table 1 illustrates these relationships.

TABLE 1

ORDERING OF REFLEX AMPLITUDE IN THE CAT

(Adapted from Chase, 1973)

MASSETERIC REFLEX

	Before 2 weeks	*6 weeks*	*Adult*
Active Sleep	highest	lowest	lowest
Quiet Sleep	intermediate	intermediate	intermediate
Wakefulness	lowest	highest	highest

DIGASTRIC REFLEX

Active Sleep	highest	lowest	lowest
Quiet Sleep	intermediate	highest	highest
Wakefulness	lowest	intermediate	intermediate

Chase points out that the neurophysiological basis for this dramatic turnabout is yet to be worked out, but the student of his work is convinced that future experiments will yield explanations from the developing brain. In fact, to paraphrase McGinty, there may be an encephalization of the neural control of wakefulness as well as of sleep. Earlier work of Chase and Sterman (1967) showed impressive negative correlations between the development of active sleep and the development of wakefulness in the cat. Others have speculated about the reciprocal role of these two organismic states in human development (Roffwarg, Muzio, and Dement, 1966; Spitz, Emde, and Metcalf, 1970). At the very least, the line of research described above offers the possibility of providing a precise neurophysiological basis for such organismic developmental discontinuities as are proposed.

C. ADDED COMPLEXITY: ENVIRONMENTAL INFLUENCE ON BRAIN GROWTH

The evidence from the cat is promising for the researchers' pursuit of an understanding of a major neurophysiological shift that occurs after the neonatal period. However, environmental influence must now be taken into account in drawing any conclusions about rates of maturation. An increasing body of research evidence indicates that we can no longer assume that postnatal brain changes occur independently from environmental influence. It has long been known that tracts in the nervous system become myelinated when they become functional and that myelinization can be stimulated or prevented by the onset of function or the lack of function respectively (Langworthy, 1933; O'Brien, 1970), but a recent and vigorous line of research has shown the effects of environmental stimulation in what is perhaps a more intriguing line of postnatal neuroanatomical development, namely on the dendritic connecting system of the neurons themselves. It has been shown repeatedly by Altman and his group (1967) and by Rosenzweig et al. (1968) that one can markedly alter the structure and function of the rat cortex by providing an enriched environment in early infancy. Compared with an impoverished condition, an enriched environment results in animals whose brains show greater weight of the cerebral cortex, higher acetyl cholinesterase throughout the brain, increased vascularity in the cortex, a higher number of newly formed glial cells, and greater dendritic branching. Most recently such research has shown a greater number of dendritic spines. The exact location of the dendritic branches and spines which are under environmental influence is now being worked out (Greenough, 1973; Rosenzweig, 1973).

CONCLUSIONS: SOME ORIENTING PROPOSITIONS AND FURTHER QUESTIONS

The evidence we have reviewed supports the potential usefulness of Spitz's theory. Our research program was therefore guided by it. In this monograph we will present our data, collected over a period of six years, data which bear on the global propositions we have derived from the genetic field theory. The propositions are:

1. Rates of behavioral and physiological development are uneven in infancy.

2. Affect behaviors are prominent indicators of times of rapid change.

3. In the determination of behavior, the proportional influence of maturation and experience will demonstrably shift toward the latter in the course of the first year.

4. Each time of rapid change will reflect a major developmental shift to a new level of organization; this shift will be manifest by the emergence of novel functions in the infant's behavioral world.

Affect behaviors became a central aspect of our investigations and, in our early work, we wondered about some other broad questions. Whether or not the onsets of smiling and stranger distress indicate times of rapid change, do these behaviors occur without antecedents? Clearly, the emergence and developmental course of affect behaviors in general deserved careful descriptive study. This was planned as a major part of our project. We also wondered about the organismic aspect of the propositions. If we measured different sectors of development and found uneven rates of development, would there be invariant sequences of change in the behavioral and physiological sectors? Would physiological changes, for example, always precede behavioral changes? Would A always precede B in the individual case? Or would we find that different sectors developed relatively independently?

Besides affect behaviors, what else should we study? What aspects of behavior and physiology should we measure in order to assess developmental organization? In the next chapter we will take up some of the reasons we chose to study states of sleep and wakefulness and the EEG. In addition, a number of behavioral variables in both infant and mother were chosen for study as part of our attempts to understand the context of the affect behaviors themselves. These will be discussed more fully in Part III.

2

OUR APPROACH: OVER-ALL STRATEGY

The central focus of our research has been the development of affect behaviors, especially smiling and crying, during the first year of life. It will come as no surprise to the reader that our organismic orientation led us to the view that the development of affects can be understood more clearly if data concerning CNS maturation, the infant's environment, and his behavior are studied together. Our approach has been to seek explanations, largely at the descriptive and correlational level, but at times we have moved to experimentation. We have studied normal infants, looking for normal patterns and sequences. Although we have been interested in physiological correlates of behavior, we have preferred to observe for long periods without interference before raising questions which require electroding or other manipulations.

SPECIAL ASPECTS OF OUR STRATEGY

Our strategy has made liberal use of movie-taking. During naturalistic observations it has been our practice to take 16 mm. movies in order to build up a library of behaviors within a given context. When findings of importance have involved behavioral observations we have prepared a film documentary for presentation purposes. Thus most of the behavioral findings to be presented in this monograph can be illustrated and studied further by reference to our film library.

Our project has involved both longitudinal and cross-sectional studies. Although the longitudinal study of individual infants is time-consuming, we believed that it was essential to our efforts. In no other way could we search for normative sequences of behavior and physiology in individual infants. In no other way could we highlight individual variability and understand more about it over time. A longitudinal approach, with an infant studied on more than two dozen visits during a year, for example, allows for the collection of "in-depth" information about families, about unreported behaviors, and about motivation. Furthermore, a considerable advantage stems from multiple observations where there is a continuing relationship with mother and family. Cross-sectional studies, each with a single observation point, allow for better control of variables and more precise statistical analysis, but the resulting group data, averaged for specific ages, creates a tendency for short-term developmental changes to be "averaged out." However, as many have pointed out (see for example, Caldwell and Hersher, 1964), because the longitudinal approach often involves many variables, relationships can be only suggested, not established. For this reason our longitudinal study, although broadly oriented by the genetic field theory, often served mainly for hypothesis generation; we therefore tried to leave time for concurrent or subsequent cross-sectional studies to answer specific questions raised by the longitudinal approach.

INITIAL SURPRISES AND THE CORRECTION OF BIAS

We began our studies with the newborn to establish some baselines. Baselines for understanding emotional organization, we thought, should consist of a full description of innate newborn capacities — capacities upon which later emotional development would be superimposed. Because of our unrealized biases we encountered some initial surprises. As we soon discovered, we were biased about *passivity* and *undifferentiation*.

In the past, we often tended to think of the human in early infancy as a relatively passive organism who reacts to stimuli and behaves in such a way as primarily to reduce stimulation. Even though there is little evidence to support this idea, it seems to pervade much of the literature of developmental psychology and psychoanalysis and has biased both research and conceptualization. That the infant is not like this is reflected in a wide span of recent research and thinking.

One such area is embryology. Actually, during embryogenesis, primordial motor cells migrate from the central canal earlier than do sensory cells. In addition, motor neurons send processes to muscle cells and establish transmission there before the sensory half of the reflex arc begins to function. These facts have led to the implication, according to the neurophysiologist Livingston (1967), that the nervous system is built for *action prior to reaction*. Another correcting influence comes from Piaget. In the last decade, his sensorimotor theory has proved to have enormous usefulness in generating research and organizing data concerning the early development of cognition and perception. At its core, this theory describes mental functions as deriving from motor actions on concrete objects (Wolff, 1960; Piaget, 1936). Finally, there is much recent human-infancy and animal research that supports the conclusion that there are definite stimulus needs, for both soothing and arousal. Such needs result in active encounters by the developing infant with his environment. (For general discussion and data reviews on this point, see R. White, 1963; Greenberg, 1965; Marler and Hamilton, 1966; Thompson and Grusec, 1970.)

Having disabused ourselves of the passivity bias, we found that a related bias rose to the surface. We became aware of our often glib use of the term "undifferentiated" when speaking of the newborn human infant. Again, we needed perspective; looking backward from birth, one has to be impressed with the amount of differentiation that has taken place in embryogenesis. But we became equally impressed with the amount of organization and endogenous control present in the first post-uterine days. First, there are the multiple, well-circumscribed, state-related behaviors in the newborn that have been so well documented by Wolff (1966) and have also been studied by many others (Prechtl, 1958; Korner, 1969; Emde and Koenig, 1969a, 1969b). Second, there are highly organized "micro-rhythms" involved in sucking, crying, and in certain stereo-typic behaviors in the newborn (Wolff, 1967). Third, there are endogenously controlled "macrorhythms" of sleep-wakefulness and activity (Kleitman and Engelmann, 1953; Sander, 1969: Sterman and Hoppenbrouwers, 1971; Gaensbauer and Emde, 1973; Emde, Swedberg, and Suzuki, 1975).

As we began to look at these organized behavior patterns, we once again became impressed with the obvious: the newborn infant not only reacts, he acts. Although he responds to external stimulation by startling or sucking, for example, most of the newborn's behavior is "spontaneous." By this we mean, along with Wolff (1966), that such behavior occurs in the absence of demonstrable internal or external stimulation. These behaviors show evidence of coordination, have rhythmic characteristics, and some degree of predictability.

These corrections took place early in our research. The result was a modified view of the newborn infant, as primarily active with a preformed organization worthy of study in its own right, and with spontaneous behaviors as a part of that organization. In terms of our baseline for affective development, we could not assume a zero point at birth. Subsequent experience is not superimposed on a formless beginning. Rather, it seemed likely that experience might serve to modulate pre-existing endogenous behaviors according to laws and operations yet to be discovered.

THE USEFULNESS OF THE CONCEPT OF STATE

As alluded to above, an important characteristic of the new-born's spontaneous behaviors is that they are related to state. Because "state" is such a pivotal concept in our methods of studying infants, it seems essential to clarify what we mean by it before we present any data. State is a "low-level" concept, subject to ready operational definition and found useful by a wide range of researchers in the physiology and behavior of human infancy (see, for example, Wolff, 1966; Hutt, Lenard, and Prechtl, 1969; Korner, 1969; Anders and Hoffman, 1973; Chase, Stern, and Walter, 1972, 1973). It is useful chiefly because it allows for prediction. Perhaps the most eloquent statement of its usefulness, as well as its limitations, is Wolff's (1960). But we must guard against the danger of hypostas-ization and remind ourselves that, like so many concepts, it is somewhat arbitrary, existing in the mind of the researcher, not in the infant. According to Prechtl et al. (1968) and Hutt, Lenard, and Prechtl (1969), state refers to constellations of certain patterns of physiological variables and/or patterns of behaviors which seem to repeat themselves and which appear to be relatively stable. Thus the concept has implications for both organization and sequencing. Perhaps because of our discovery of our initial biases, we have often found it useful to think of the concept of state as referring to a group of variables at a given point in development which determine readiness to act on the one hand, and readiness to react on the other.

Because some spontaneous state-related activities were found to resemble later affect expressions, we spent a consid-erable amount of time in the study of state patterns. Our operational criteria for newborn behavioral states are pre-sented in Table A (see Appendix). We found that these states were easily judged and consistently yielded high interrater agreement (see Emde and Koenig, 1969b; Emde, McCartney, and Harmon, 1971; Bernstein, Emde, and Campos, 1973).

The correlation of behavioral states with physiological patterning was also studied (Emde and Metcalf, 1970). Later, we participated in the designation of a standard international system for the coding and labeling of physiological and behavioral states of sleep and wakefulness (Anders, Emde, and Parmelee, 1971).

The discussion up to now has dealt with the newborn. What about the state concept at later ages? It is worthwhile considering this question to sharpen our thinking and to avoid hypostasization. The amount of scientific literature dealing with state-related variables drops off precipitously after the newborn period. Notwithstanding the unrepresentative amount of research which has been devoted to the newborn period, one gets the impression that the concept of state is in fact much less useful in studying the older child, for the following reasons. First, the concept has been most useful in studying sleep, and sleep states (especially the REM states) decrease in amount and importance as wakefulness increases. Second, with postnatal forebrain maturation there is increasing inhibition of the behavioral activity which is so prominent a feature of neonatal sleep states. In older children, behavioral states are often not clearly distinguishable during sleep; hence, physiological variables, especially as indexed by the EEG, are emphasized. Sleep researchers, studying older children and adults, use the concept of sleep "stages" (related to specific EEG criteria) rather than sleep "states." Third, when the focus of research shifts to waking states, most psychological studies are carried out when the subjects are alert and attentive, when psychological differences in readiness to respond are complex, subtle, and less likely to show obvious physiological correlates. Hence, readiness to respond is more likely to be defined in terms of attitudes, set, cognitive style, and psychological structures.[1]

[1]Nonetheless, in spite of the negative view presented concerning the usefulness of the concept of state at a later age, it remains an intriguing idea that the behavioral-physiological states of infancy might be antecedents of, or contribute to, the later

WHY STUDY SLEEP?

Why study sleep? The simplest answer is that the human being, after birth, spends two thirds of his early existence sleeping. Anyone seriously interested in studying the infant is naturally directed toward his sleep. But does it have anything to do with his developing behavioral world? Is not sleep his "natural state of rest" (Freud, 1900, 1911) and therefore static and of little interest to a project focusing on affect development?

As the reader might suspect, recent research has changed our attitude about sleep. It has become an exciting area of developmental research, with the promise of new and significant knowledge. The newborn human is not "at rest" during sleep, but is behaviorally active, with a rather extensive repertoire of well-organized sleep behaviors (Wolff, 1959). Frowns and smiles are among a variety of facial expressions and bodily movements which intrigue the researcher. Sleep activity is such that if one measures the infant's behavioral output by means of a sensitive air-filled crib mattress, the amount found during sleep can exceed that observed during his periods of noncrying wakefulness.[2]

---

development of moods and/or patterns of orienting reactions (see, for example, Graham and Jackson, 1970). Certainly the hypothesis of a basic rest-activity cycle influencing daytime as well as nighttime activity at all ages is no longer speculative (see Kripke, 1972; Othmer, Hayden, and Segelbaum, 1969; Globus, 1966; Sterman and Hoppenbrouwers, 1971).

[2]We conducted an exploratory study in conjunction with Dr. Louis Sander, who was kind enough to allow us to observe and film a 15-day-old infant being studied on his activity interaction monitor (A.I.M.) (Sander and Julia, 1966). The A.I.M., devised by Sander and his group to study infants under different caretaking conditions for a continuous two-month period after birth (Sander et al., 1970), has the advantage of providing continuous monitoring of activity. A feeding-to-feeding period was observed in our joint study. An observer made minute-by-minute observations of state and associated behaviors. A second observer took a 16 mm. movie with time samples for later study and independent rating. The A.I.M. output was then matched with judgments of behavioral state made from film and direct observation. This study provided the basis for our assertion about the amount of activity possible during sleep.

But the baby's sleep is not *all* active. There are at least two "types" of sleep, separable into "active" and "quiet." A new era of modern sleep research began with the discovery by Aserinsky and Kleitman (1955) that newborn infants alternated between periods of activity and quiesence and that in sleep the active period occurred with rapid eye movements (REM sleep) and the quiescent period occurred without rapid eye movements (NREM sleep). Although similar observations had been reported earlier in the Russian literature (Denisova and Figurin, 1929), it was Aserinsky and Kleitman's finding, subsequently generalized to adult humans and mammals, which stimulated an enormous amount of multidisciplinary behavioral-biological research (see, e.g., Chase, 1973). In what is now a classic paper, Roffwarg, Muzio, and Dement (1966) reviewed research findings concerning the ontogeny of these types of sleep. Far from being static, sleep evidences rapid developmental change. Roffwarg et al. estimated that 50% of the neonate's total sleep is REM sleep whereas in the year-old child REM sleep is 30%, and in the adolescent only 20%. But why such a high amount of REM sleep in early infancy, they wondered. After reviewing another body of research literature suggesting that the young organism was programmed not so much to shut out stimulation as to require it for neural growth, they offered what has become known as the "ontogenetic hypothesis" for the biological function of REM sleep. According to this hypothesis, early in ontogeny, REM sleep, with all of its behavioral and neurophysiological activation, serves to provide a source of endogenous afferentation needed for central nervous system growth. They reasoned that this afferentation was particularly important in the altricial human whose immaturity at birth precludes much activity during wakefulness.

More recently, attention has been directed to the development of NREM or quiet sleep. This form of sleep increases during infancy, and there is some suggestion that it is correlated with the postnatal maturation of forebrain inhibitory centers (Sterman and Clemente, 1962; McGinty, 1971). Perhaps the most important fact about quiet sleep is that, in contrast to active REM sleep, it evidences great *qualitative* change during the first year. Parmelee et al. (1967) have pointed out that active REM sleep can be regarded as a more primitive state than quiet sleep. They believe that the changing postnatal physiology of quiet sleep may reflect basic maturational events in higher centers which are fundamentally related to the development of wakefulness.

Such is the remarkable change in our attitude toward sleep which has taken place in the span of less than two decades. Sleep is the arena for both quantitative and qualitative changes which undoubtedly reflect basic developmental shifts in central nervous system organization and in total organismic functioning. Thus, even though it is in wakefulness that novelty is experienced, that our world is expanded, that we change and are most changed, and that most learning takes place, it may be sleep which offers a more accessible mirror of the rapid organismic changes of early development. It is no longer useful merely to regard sleep as the negative aspect of wakefulness. In fact, sleep development may provide a key to understanding the development of wakefulness itself, where major physiological changes over time are less evident.

WHY STUDY THE EEG?

Although Caton made the first observations of brain electrical activity (1875), it was not until 1929 that the psychiatrist Hans Berger first recorded the human EEG from the scalp. Since then, the EEG has been used primarily in clinical neurology, and, more recently, in sleep research. Its usefulness in these fields has been strictly empirical. Changing EEG patterns are correlated with neuropathological conditions and with alterations in states of consciousness. Although the EEG is generally thought to correlate with cerebral functioning, our understanding of the neurophysiological mechanisms underlying the wiggles obtained from the scalp electrodes is meager. There has been considerable study during the last 50 years, but it is not yet clear how or where the rhythmic oscillations originate (Kiloh, McComas, and Osselton, 1972).

In view of this uncertainty, why should we be concerned with the EEG? The first reason follows from the importance of sleep. Not only does sleep change dramatically in amounts and form during infancy, its EEG characteristics also change. Unlike other parameters used in scoring sleep states — for example, behavioral activity, eye movements, respiratory patterns, and muscle tone — the EEG evidences the onset of new patterns after birth. In other words, there are distinct qualitative changes. Patterns not present in the days after birth appear in the course of infant development and remain into and through adulthood. These changes undoubtedly reflect brain maturation (Dreyfus-Brisac, 1966; Metcalf, 1970). Questions logically follow from this fact. Do these EEG events occur in any fixed relation to the onset of social smiling or to the onset of stranger distress? Do they cluster with other changes and give support to the notion of organismic change? At the time of planning our study, we had intriguing data from Dr. David Metcalf which suggested that there might be such a general temporal coincidence of events. Some EEG pattern shifts occurred early, around two months, and some later, around six months or afterwards. A longitudinal study was needed to investigate time relationships in individual cases.

A second reason for being interested in EEG data follows from speculations about the meaning of the changing patterns themselves. Two of them, the development of sustained slow waves during sleep onset and the development of hypersynchronous drowsiness, affect the transition between wakefulness and sleep and would seem to have implications for the maturation of central nervous system arousal mechanisms. Another event, the development of sleep spindles, may reflect a new capacity of the brain for integrating excitatory and inhibitory systems. Although the functional significance of sleep spindles is unknown, attention has been drawn to them because their onset is affected by metabolic disturbances such as hypothyroidism (Schultz et al., 1968) and untreated phenyl-ketonuria (Schulte et al., 1973).

The development of K-complexes is another EEG event which has offered grounds for intriguing speculations. K-complexes occur in quiet sleep and have been found to be associated with an increase in heart rate and changes in other autonomic nervous system variables (Johnson and Karpen, 1968; Johnson, 1973). This development may represent another qualitative shift in the maturation of arousal mechanisms. Does it reflect a change in limbic system regulation? Equally intriguing is a speculation of Metcalf, Mondale, and Butler (1971), who noted the similarity in form of the spontaneous K-complex and the sensory evoked response, and suggested that the onset of the former may represent the infant's enhanced ability to process information and maintain a mental experience.

3

SAMPLES, SCHEDULES, AND SCALES

This chapter is intended to serve as a guide for understanding how we went about our research. In the interest of readability, tables of criteria and reliability have been placed in an appendix (see p. 167).

Our selection of study infants required screening for normality. In virtually all instances, the data reported in this monograph were derived from infants who met the following criteria at the time of birth: (1) no defined medical complications during pregnancy, labor, or delivery; (2) a one-minute Apgar rating of 7 or above and a five-minute Apgar rating of 9 or above; (3) an estimated gestational age of 38-42 weeks; (4) a birth weight of 2700-3600 grams. Cases in which these criteria were not fulfilled are specifically identified in subsequent chapters. The rationale for our criteria of normality emerged from the extensive studies of Lubchenco and co-workers (1966, 1972) and Drage et al. (1966).

INITIAL LONGITUDINAL STUDY

In an initial longitudinal study, 16 pregnant women of middle- to upper-class status were recruited from prenatal hospital clinics and discussion groups. Postnatally, both mothers and infants were seen once a week for three and one half months. Four cases had to be dropped from the final data analysis because of gaps in the schedule of contacts. Of the remaining 12 mothers, nine were primiparous and three had one other child. Of their infants, six were male and six female.

Biweekly home visits were made by two observers for maternal interviews and infant testing; these alternated with biweekly laboratory visits for EEG and polygraphic recordings. This study was primarily designed for another purpose, to test certain ideas of John Benjamin's concerning the "stimulus barrier" in early infancy. A report of that aspect of the research has been published elsewhere (Tennes et al., 1972). For this monograph, the relevant aspects of the study were the observations of affect behaviors in the context of the infant's day, and the perceptual and neurological testing. Some of the information obtained from this study is summarized in subsequent chapters. Some of it has been replicated and expanded in our longitudinal study of the first year.

Longitudinal Study of the First Year

The main focus of this monograph is a longitudinal study of 14 infants throughout the first postnatal year. It began after the first study was completed and, in each case, contact extended from the mother's third trimester of pregnancy until the end of the infant's first postnatal year. Nine women in our sample were chosen from prenatal clinics, and they recruited the other five. Educationally, two mothers were high school graduates, six had a partial college education, and six were college graduates. None were working when the study began, although two engaged in some part-time work at some time during the year. Of the fathers, four were high school graduates (salesman, clerk, construction worker, small businessman), three were college graduates (salesmen, teacher), four were graduate students (law, engineering, medicine), and three were physicians.

Our experience in the first longitudinal study led us to make certain alterations in our selection procedures for the year-long longitudinal study. Because we wanted to supplement our observations with accurate mothers' reports, and because of our desire to minimize maternal anxiety in what was an essentially infant-centered biobehavioral study, we made an effort to secure second-born children for study whenever possible. We reasoned that maternal anxiety and uncertainty about birth, rearing, and family role expectations would be much less in women who had already had one child than in primiparas. On the other hand, more than two children would add another kind of complexity to our observational field. Since we wanted to study infants for an entire year, during our enrollment interviews we were explicit about the need for commitment, giving each potential volunteer the schedule of requirements for our study. We explained that any benefit to them would be derived from participating in a research study of normal development, seeing a variety of developmental tests performed on their infants throughout the first year, and receiving a brief motion picture of their infant at the end of the year. All candidates for our study understood that, in addition to 10 or more home visits by our research team, participation would involve at least 13 half-day visits to our laboratory for EEG-polygraphic recording and two visits for playroom sessions. We asked the women to discuss this information with their husbands if husbands were not present at our first interview. During a second visit shortly thereafter, if both husband and wife agreed to participate, we formally enrolled them in the study, obtained their informed consent, and began our interview by asking about their expectations of the baby. The success of our enrollment procedure is indicated by the fact that all 14 cases taken into the study completed the entire year.

All mothers were assessed as being relatively high in competence and low in anxiety. Of the 14 infants, three were first-born children, nine were second-born, and two were third-born; eight were female and six male.

Observations were made twice a month, instead of four times a month as in the first longitudinal study. Again, home visits alternated with laboratory visits for EEG and polygraphic recordings. In all instances, the EEG-polygraph visit occurred within the week following a home visit.

A. PROCEDURE

1. Home Visits. Monthly home visits were made by two and occasionally three investigators. Visits lasted about one and a half hours and included a maternal interview, a filmed social-interaction series, informal observations of mother-infant interaction, Piaget tests for object permanence, and, if time and the infant's state permitted, other tests of infant development.

Maternal interviews were conducted according to an interview schedule, and recorded on a portable tape recorder; the tapes were later transcribed verbatim. The interview itself always began with an open-ended inquiry about changes since our previous visit. After a detailed follow-up of the mother's spontaneous account of changes, the interview continued and always included the following topics:

A detailed review of the previous 24 hours. This inquiry was a modification of the Gesell and Ilg behaviour-day chart method (1943); instead of having mothers keep records of daily sleep times, waking times, and feeding times, we asked them to recall such details for the previous day and night. We then asked specific questions designed to elicit data about what would have been considered "modal" for the previous week. In a pilot case, in which we used the Gesell mother-charting method, we observed that a highly intelligent and motivated mother found it difficult and tedious to keep such daily records over the months demanded by our study. On the other hand, we discovered that she could easily and accurately remember the previous 24 hours and, if we asked about what was typical and what was not, about the longest sleep period

and the longest wakeful period, we could accurately recon-
struct a typical day and night for the previous week. An
additional advantage of this procedure was that as mothers
described the previous 24 hours, data about many other areas
on our interview schedule would be given spontaneously and
could be followed up. Questions about the quality of sleep and
wakefulness were included in our follow-up. In addition, we
inquired about the quality and amount of feedings, about
whether they seemed satisfactory for mother and infant, about
whether the nature of feedings had changed, and about
whether breast, bottle, solids, or cup feedings had been
introduced.

*A review of the infant's social development since the last
visit.* Our primary interest was in the infant's differential
responsiveness to people. We asked: Does your baby react any
differently to you compared with anyone else? Compared with
father, compared with sibling? If so, how? We also asked: Do
you think your baby knows you? How? Any information about
affective responses was followed up in detail. Information
about what the infant liked and disliked was also obtained.

*A specific review of the infant's fussiness and distress
behaviors.*

*A review of any illnesses, medications given to the infant,
visits to the doctor, trips outside the home, occasions when the
infant was taken on visits or was left with others.* A review of
the reaction to the last EEG visit.

A review of anything related to teething.

Specific questions about the infant's sleep environment —
whether it had been changed since our last visit, whether there
were any sleep disturbances.

*Specific questions about separations and responses to stran-
gers.* A modification of the Schaffer and Emerson (1964)
interview schedule for separation experiences was used. We
asked about the infant's response to being passed by in the
room, to being left alone in the room, to being left alone in the
house, and to being left with a baby-sitter. We also ascer-

tained the infant's initial state at these times — whether he was alert, tired, asleep, fretful, or otherwise. Questions about stranger responses concerned the degree of avoidance, if any; the degree of distress, if any; and the context of the response, in terms of both the situation and the state of the infant.

A review of family events since the last visit. We also asked, before concluding the interview, if there were any other changes.

All testing was filmed by means of a 16 mm. movie camera with a telephoto-zoom lens so that the camera could be positioned about 20 feet from the infant and the photographer could be hidden behind it.

During the first three months, testing included neurological assessment of transitory reflexes and a sampling of responsiveness to visual, auditory, kinesthetic, and tactile stimulation. Smiling was elicited in a wide variety of stimulus conditions, including a comparison of the mother's face with unfamiliar faces. However, this aspect of the infant's behavior was not emphasized since it had been thoroughly explored at two-week intervals in the first longitudinal study (Tennes et al., 1972).

For the four- and five-months-old infant, our social-interaction series consisted of the following sequence: (A) Mother leaves, (B) Stranger 1 approaches, (C) Mother returns, (D) A period during which the infant has an opportunity to compare the mother's and the stranger's nodding faces. At six months and thereafter, the sequence was lengthened to include a second stranger who approached with the mother present. At the beginning of the series the infant was seated in a highchair and, as the sequence progressed, at least 30 seconds of observation time was allowed between each of the interactions listed above, to allow for delayed responses. The stranger entered from an adjacent room, and (1) approached silently to within three feet of the infant, nodding the face; (2) said, "Hello, baby -----, how are you?" in a low voice; (3) gently picked up the baby. Each action was gauged so as to take approximately the same amount of time. The complete social-interaction series took eight to 10 minutes and could be encompassed in a continuously running 400-foot roll of film. Tests for object permanence (in Piaget's sense) were also filmed and are described below, in Chapter 9.

2. Visits for Electrophysiological Recording. At two weeks of age, and at monthly birthdays thereafter, infants were brought by their mothers for a morning's session in our electrophysiological laboratory. There, in a room especially designed for infant research by Dr. David Metcalf, they were prepared for recording during a morning's nap which, as often as possible, began with a feeding by the mother and continued for two to three hours. Electrophysiological recording was done by means of a 16-channel Model 78 Grass EEG-Polygraph Recording System in which seven channels were used for EEG, four channels for recording eye movements (EOG), one channel for submental electromyogram (EMG), one channel for respiration, one channel for a special-events marker, one channel for a time-code generator, and one channel left blank. During the first three months, Beckman Ag-Cl electrodes were used to improve recording quality during feeding, crying, and other periods of vigorous body activity. Electrodes were placed at International System locations Cz, A2, F8, T6, F4, and C4. Time constants of the amplifiers were as follows: EOG, 0.3 sec.; EEG and EMG, 0.12 sec. A DC amplifier was used to record respiration which was transmitted from a bellows-pneumograph attached to the infant. During recordings, an EEG technician monitored the polygraph and wrote down intermittent behavioral observations transmitted to her through earphones from an observer near the infant who whispered into a microphone.

3. Playroom Visits. At six months and 12 months of age, mothers brought their infants to our playroom instead of our visiting their homes. The playroom visits, like the home visits, included the filmed social-interaction series, the Piaget testing, and the maternal interview, but also included developmental testing. Such testing relied on the Buhler and Hetzer

(1935) and Cattell (1940) tests. Unfortunately, the more complete and better standardized Bayley (1969) test of mental and motor development did not become available to us until after our study was under way.[1] As in the home, playroom testing was filmed, but from an adjacent room specially designed for photographing all aspects of the playroom through one-way glass. Playroom visits were included not only for convenience of developmental testing, but also to see if there were important differences in context which could influence responsiveness to the stranger in our social-interaction series.

B. ANALYSIS OF DATA

1. Rating Scales. Three major rating scales were devised for use by judges who read the typed transcripts of maternal interviews. These scales quantified dimensions of fussiness, separation distress, and stranger distress. Each scale ranged from an absent (0) to a maximal (4 or 5) rating (see Table B in Appendix).

In the initial longitudinal study, smiles were rated on a 1-4 scale on the basis of written descriptions of the infant's behavior during home visits (see Table C in Appendix).

In addition, detailed ratings were derived from film analysis. Judgments were made of responsiveness in a variety of dimensions, including facial expressions, motor activity, and direction of response; global impressions of the presence or absence of stranger and separation distress were also rated. The primary rating scale for the social-interaction series is presented in Table D (see Appendix). A secondary scale of intensity of separation distress and stranger distress was mathematically derived from the primary ratings from the films.

[1] Infants were tested at six and 12 months of age with the Cattell Developmental Test (1940). Rank order correlations were calculated between developmental quotients at the two ages and the onset of early fussiness, the onset of stranger distress, and the onset of separation distress. None of these correlations was significant. All infants tested in the normal range at both ages.

For this scale, only items of high interjudge reliability on the primary scale were used (see Table E in Appendix).

In addition to these scales, other categories of information were abstracted from the transcribed interviews by independent raters who knew nothing about any of the hypotheses of the study. These categories included the presence or absence of a variety of teething symptoms as well as the number of teeth, the presence or absence of any illness, the presence or absence of any feeding changes, and the presence or absence of any stressful events. The raters also abstracted sleep, wakefulness, and feeding for the typical week preceding the visit, and quantified sleep and wakefulness at two-hour intervals throughout the previous 24-hours.[2]

2. *Reliability.* The fussiness scale was used in both our initial longitudinal study and our longitudinal study of the first year. In the initial study (Tennes et al., 1972), three judges made independent ratings; perfect agreement was difficult to obtain, but for all judgments there was 98% agreement within one point on our six-point scale. In our longitudinal study of the first year, interrater reliability was higher; two independent judges reached 92% perfect agreement.

Interjudge reliability for the separation and stranger distress scales was assessed for five of our 14 infants. Reliability percent for complete agreement on the separation distress

---

[2] Because such a mass of detailed interview material from mothers was available, we thought we might be able to extract information about individual differences in the babies' affect expressions and other traits as well. On a *post hoc* basis, we devised several versions of a rating scale for traits, taking common elements from previously reported infant trait scales (Gesell and Ames, 1937; Kagan and Moss, 1962; Thomas et al., 1963; Schaefer and Bayley, 1963; Escalona, 1968). Raters were then instructed to make judgments from the typed transcripts of maternal interviews. However, interrater agreement was not high enough on any dimension of this scale to warrant further pursuit of this aspect of our study. Whether our failure was due to the inherent difficulties in seeing temporal continuity of traits in the rapidly changing infant, or to our *post hoc* method, is uncertain. We believe that any future work in this area should include a prospective design with periodic observations of both mother and infant, as well as specifically focused interviews with mothers. In retrospect, our approach was naïve, especially in the light of the issues and methods so well set forth by Escalona (1953, 1968).

scalé was 91%, and on the stranger distress scale was 93%.

Because films of the social-interaction series contained crucial observational data, all judgments from films were made by two independent raters. This task involved the rating of nearly 3600 feet of film for each of the 14 infants. Interjudge reliability percentages for complete agreement are presented in Table F (see Appendix). Agreement was consistently high (90% or greater) for global ratings of separation and stranger distress. Other agreement percentages were adequate, except for the rating of motor activity, which was consistently low. Motor activity ratings were therefore not included in the intensity rating scale which was derived from the primary ratings.

Reliabilities for other categories of data obtained from maternal interviews are presented in Table G (see Appendix). Judgments by two independent raters were obtained for two cases, and, since they appeared to be adequate, the other cases were not rated.

3. Statistical Analysis. In all of our data analysis we gave primary emphasis to a clear description of phenomena. Typically, we started with scattergram plots of time-dependent variables before correlations were calculated. Often simple descriptions could answer important questions about necessary sequences as we compared one case with another. Rank order correlations were often calculated in our longitudinal work because of the advantage of being able to rank-order time of onset of specific variables and correlate them with other variables. Wherever convenient we used Pearson Product Moment correlations, even with rated items. Even though the use of such a parametric procedure on rating scales violates a major statistical assumption, Cohen (1965) has pointed out that advantages outweigh disadvantages. Correlational statistics are the ones most used in our longitudinal study. In our analysis of cross-sectional data, we have made more extensive use of Tau statistics for analyzing differences between groups. In these instances we have employed parametric and nonparametric procedures as appropriate.

PART II

SLEEP, WAKEFULNESS, AND THE EEG

4

AN OVERVIEW OF SLEEP AND
WAKEFULNESS DURING
THE FIRST YEAR

The newborn spends twice as much time sleeping as adults
do. From previous estimates, we know that this difference is
much diminished by the end of the first year (Roffwarg, Muzio,
and Dement, 1966). Given the nature of our study, an obvious
question emerged: In the first postnatal year, does sleep
decline steadily while wakefulness increases steadily? Or are
changes uneven and discontinuous?

Table 2 summarizes data on the total amount of daily sleep
during the first postnatal year. Except for the newborn period,
information in the table comes from maternal interviews in
our longitudinal studies. Values at each age are taken to
represent average values for the previous week. Although these
data are derived from maternal interviews and not from direct
observations, certain features give us confidence in their
usefulness. First, the mean values for the first three months of
the year-long study (italicized) are in striking agreement
with the values at the same ages in the initial 14-week study.
Second, our results also agree with those previously reported by
Parmelee, Wenner, and Schulz (1964) for a 16-week longitudinal study.

Figure 1 graphically represents these changes in terms of the
mean hours of daily wakefulness. A best-fitting curve is
sketched in the figure to illustrate what available data suggest

49

TABLE 2

MEAN TOTAL DAILY SLEEP DURING THE FIRST POSTNATAL YEAR
Values in Hours

Age	Cross-sectional Study N = 20		Initial 14-wk. Study N = 12		Year-long Study N = 14		Parmelee, Wenner, and Schulz (1964) Longitudinal Study N = 46	
	Mean	S.D.	Mean	S.D.	Mean	S.D.	Mean	S.D.
1 day	18.46	2.07						
2 weeks			17.90	1.36			16.25	1.60
1 month			15.39	1.53	15.60	1.88	15.43	1.60
6 weeks			16.23	1.39				
2 months			15.40	2.21	15.35	1.61	15.42	1.70
10 weeks			15.45	2.28				
3 months			15.55	1.64	15.43	2.41	15.11	1.48
14 weeks			14.80	2.05				
4 months					15.55	2.17		
5 months					15.24	1.93		
6 months					14.94	2.12		
7 months					14.27	1.59		
8 months					14.16	1.59		
9 months					14.33	1.49		
10 months					14.81	1.35		
11 months					14.26	1.28		
12 months					14.38	0.84		

about the development of wakefulness. The visual impression given by this curve is of two increases, each followed by a plateau. Statistical analysis supports the visual impression. Using independent data from the three studies, a significant difference was found between the values of mean daily wakefulness at one month and the lower values at two weeks, and the still lower values at one day ($p < .01$, 2-tailed t test in each instance). In the data from the year-long longitudinal study, although an analysis of variance on values for the entire year was not significant ($F = 1.46$), daily wakefulness at seven months was found to be significantly higher than at four months ($t = 2.80$; $p < .05$, 2-tailed t test). In addition, all values after seven months were significantly higher than all values before four months. On the other hand, presumably

MEAN HOURS OF DAILY WAKEFULNESS DURING THE FIRST YEAR

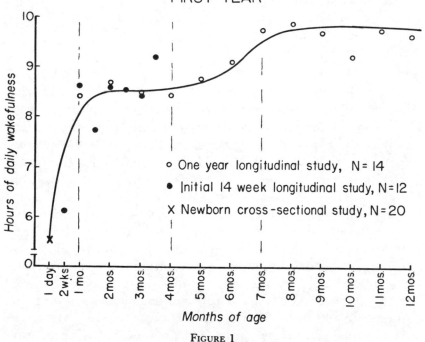

○ One year longitudinal study, N = 14

● Initial 14 week longitudinal study, N = 12

X Newborn cross-sectional study, N = 20

Months of age

FIGURE 1

because of the very much lower amount of wakefulness at two weeks, the analysis of variance on the 14-week longitudinal study was highly significant ($F = 3.34$; $p < .01$, 2-tailed t test).

An evaluation of individual data from the year-long study revealed a tendency for large increases to occur during the four-to-nine months period. In all 14 infants the largest monthly increase in amount of wakefulness occurred during this period, 10 of the 14 showing the largest increase in the narrower five-to-eight-months period (median age, six months). The early period of increase in wakefulness could not be evaluated from individual case data because of our lack of a baseline for the newborn period.

In short, this analysis suggested two times of quantitative change, one during the first two months and one from about five to eight months. But what about other changes in each period? What about changes in day-night distribution? What about changes in sleep and wakefulness? These questions guided what we did next in analyzing our data. We will take up each period separately.

A. THE EARLY PERIOD

Dramatic changes are evident in the day-night distribution of sleep and wakefulness during the early postnatal months. Numerous investigators have systematically documented the absence of day-night variations in sleep and wakefulness during the first week of life (Hellbrügge, 1960; Kleitman, 1963; Parmelee, Wenner, and Schulz, 1964; Sander and Julia, 1966). Then with increasing age, periods of wakefulness become longer and show a tendency to become concentrated during the daytime. Figures 2 and 3 (data taken from our year-long study and our initial longitudinal study) illustrate the progressive development of a predominance of daytime wakefulness. The average amount of sleep for each two-hour period of the 24-hour day is represented at each age of our longitudinal studies. The figures show a clear pattern of daytime wakefulness by two months of age in the year-long study and by 10 weeks of age in the initial study. At these ages, and afterwards, wakefulness seems clearly predominant during the day in a way it has not been before. Statistical analysis revealed that the change occurred even earlier. A Friedman two-way analysis of variance (Siegel, 1956) did not support the inference of an uneven distribution of sleep across the 24-hour period at two weeks of age, but the same test was significant beyond the .01 level at one month and after in both longitudinal studies. Using another statistical approach, differences between amounts of day and night sleep became significant by the first month of observation ($p <$ .01, 2-tailed t test in each longitudinal study).

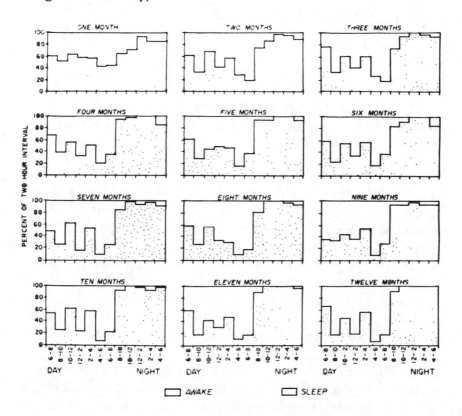

FIGURE 2

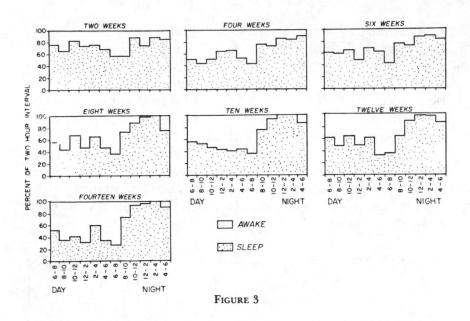

FIGURE 3

The average longest sleep period for the modal week is another interesting measure which changes during this early period. Figure 4 illustrates a dramatic increase in the infant's ability to sustain long periods of sleep during the early part of the year. The longest mean period of wakefulness does not increase nearly so much during the first year and is characterized by relatively high standard deviations at each age. For the reader with a special interest, Table H (see Appendix) lists means and standard deviations for hours of daytime sleep, nighttime sleep, and longest periods of wakefulness throughout the first year.

These data correspond to those of Parmelee, Wenner, and Schulz (1964), who studied 46 infants and found that their average longest sleep period doubled during their first four postnatal months. These investigators also found that the average longest wakeful period was more variable. It is noteworthy that, on the basis of their review of anatomic changes in the brain, they concluded that an "ability to sustain longer periods of sleep and wakefulness must be dependent on an in-

AVERAGE LONGEST SLEEP PERIOD

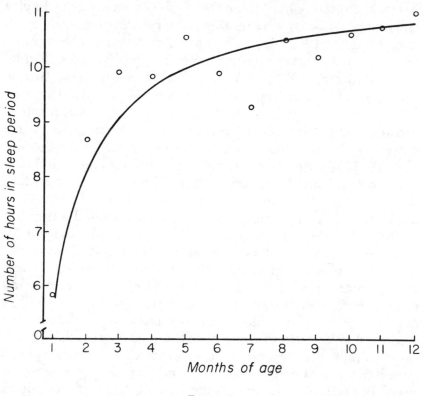

FIGURE 4

creasingly higher level of organization of the central nervous system" (p. 580).

Thus quantitative changes during this early period are dramatic. But what about qualitative changes? Is there a major difference in kind between the sleep and wakefulness of the newborn and the sleep and wakefulness of the normal infant of about two months? We think some evidence from our work favors an affirmative answer.

When we began our newborn studies, we ran head on into difficulties. We were seeking to ascertain relative amounts of sleep and wakefulness after birth. But it was often quite difficult to tell when a newborn fell asleep, a difficulty encountered not only by mothers observed during early feedings (Emde and Koenig, 1969a) but also by researchers trying to standardize and codify the onset of sleep (Anders, Emde, and Parmelee, 1971). We found that what some would consider to be "nonsleep states" (occasional periods of drowsiness, nutritional sucking, fussing, and crying), others would consider to be REM "sleep" because of an electrophysiological pattern indistinguishable from the latter state (Emde and Metcalf, 1970). Because of this complexity, we concluded that it was difficult to characterize the newborn's states according to the simple dichotomy of sleep-wakefulness. Instead, we used a scheme of 12 state categories which included a number of "behaviorally undifferentiated REM states" (see Chapter 2). Then, for purposes of estimating the quantity of sleep, we relied on a number of different cross-sectional studies. These are summarized in Table I (see Appendix). It was reassuring to find that when average amounts of states were expressed as percentages of observation time, values were similar across studies, despite differences in conditions of observation. From these studies, our best estimate was that the newborn spends about two thirds of his first postnatal days in some form of sleep. But our decision about what we called "sleep" remained somewhat arbitrary: eye closure was a criterion, even though we knew that sometimes REM electrophysiology occurred with eyes open.

But from the developmental point of view, changes occur. The boundaries between sleep and wakefulness become more clear-cut after two to three months. What we referred to as "behaviorally undifferentiated REM states" become much less prominent after early infancy.[1]

[1] The rates of decline of the behaviorally undifferentiated REM states have not been studied. Since the studies reported above were carried out we have adopted a method similar to that of Parmelee, Wenner, and Schulz (1964) and Anders and Zangen (1972) for scoring sleep states. This method includes a way of quantifying transitional states now referred to in a standardized international system as

Another line of evidence about a qualitative difference came from a detailed look at the newborn's sleep-wakefulness cycle. Contrary to our expectations from the literature, we found that there is a rhythmic organization in the infant's sleep and wakefulness. One study found evidence of a sleep-wakefulness cycle of about three and one half hours duration in one- and two-day-old demand-fed infants (Gaensbauer and Emde, 1973). Another study found evidence of a similar cycle in the first 10 hours following birth, evidence which was especially convincing since the cycle occurred in the absence of feeding (Emde, Swedberg, and Suzuki, 1975). The newborn's sleep-wakefulness cycle is in addition to the basic rest-activity cycle which is expressed in the alternation of active REM and quiet NREM sleep (Kleitman, 1963). The basic rest-activity cycle has been well studied in premature and full-term normal infants (Dreyfus-Brisac, 1966, 1970; Parmelee, Wenner, and Schulz, 1964; Sterman and Hoppenbrouwers, 1971); it undergoes a gradual development, gradually increasing from 45-50 minutes in the newborn to an average of 90 minutes in the older child and adult. The infant's sleep-wakefulness cycle, on the other hand, so far as we know, does not gradually increase. This three-and-one-half-hour cycle becomes "entrained" or synchronized with the feeding activities of the caretaker. In addition, as wakefulness increases during the day, this cycle becomes obscured by the longer day-night alternation of sleep and wakefulness. For this reason, the shorter neonatal sleep-wakefulness cycle is usually prominent only in the first week or two. Sterman and Hoppenbrouwers (1971) consider the sleep-wakefulness cycle exclusively in the sense of the day-night alternation; consequently, they describe it as beginning around two to three months after birth. But they take special account of the qualitative differences in sleep

---

"indeterminate sleep" (Anders, Emde, and Parmelee, 1971). The method also involves separate scoring of behavioral activity, eye movements and patterns of respiration, EEG and EMG from polygraphic records; computer techniques are used for data analysis.

and wakefulness between the newborn period and the period of later infancy. Indeed, on the basis of neurophysiological considerations, Sterman (personal communication) has argued that because of such differences it is difficult to compare the "wakefulness" of the newborn with the wakefulness observed after three months.

B. A LATER PERIOD

Qualitative changes in infant sleep and wakefulness after three months are difficult to evaluate in any way comparable to the ways of evaluating changes before this time. The later period of infancy has been studied less by ourselves and others, and we have had less opportunity to apply cross-sectional and short-term longitudinal studies to the later period of wakefulness increase and afterwards. But even more important, the differentiation of wakefulness becomes dominated more by cognitive and experiential factors and less by general organismic factors. Changes in the cognitive realm will be discussed in Chapter 9. In addition, later changes in the organization of emotional expressions and of heart rate will be discussed in Chapters 10, 11, and 13.

After three months there are no dramatic changes in the distribution of sleep and wakefulness (see Figure 2). Changes in the sleep EEG do take place after three months and are discussed in the next chapter.

CONCLUSION: AN IMPRESSION OF AN UNEVEN DEVELOPMENT

From the evidence we have presented, it appears that developmental changes in sleep and wakefulness occur at an uneven rate. The most striking changes occur during the first two to three months. Not only is there a marked increase in the amount of wakefulness during this early period, but there is a consolidation of a day-night pattern and a rapid increase in the ability to sustain long periods of sleep. The boundaries between sleep and wakefulness become less ambiguous during this time, and these and other characteristics give rise to an impression of qualitative differences between the sleep and wakefulness in the newborn period and these same states after two to three months. Another increase in wakefulness appears to occur between five to eight months, but there is considerable individual variability with respect to this phenomenon.

5

AN OVERVIEW OF THE EEG
DURING THE FIRST YEAR

As described in Chapter 2, the EEG changes dramatically during the first year. New patterns develop, and the literature suggests that these patterns have important functional significance. Early ones include sleep spindles and the patterns of falling asleep quietly with a slower, mixed frequency EEG (usually referred to as quiet or NREM sleep onset). Later ones include hypersynchronous drowsy activity and K-complexes. These patterns, not present in the newborn, appear and then remain in some form throughout the life span. Would their appearance be related to the onset of affect expressions? We hoped our longitudinal study would provide answers.

Details of our recording technique have been presented in Chapter 3. EEGs were obtained during a morning's laboratory visit scheduled within a week following our monthly visits. All records were scored by Dr. David Metcalf, using his published rating scales for spindle development (1970), K-complex development (Metcalf, Mondale, and Butler, 1971) and hypersynchronous drowsy development (personal communication). These scales are presented in the Appendix (Tables J, K, and L).

In presenting our results, we will first look at questions about clusters of changes. Do EEG changes cluster at certain times? Do EEG and affect behavior changes cluster at the same times? Such clustering of changes would be predicted by the genetic field theory. Secondly, we will look at questions about regularities in sequences. Are there necessary or consistent sequences, with one change predictably preceding another? A finding of regularities in sequences between sectors would be significant evidence in the search for underlying mechanisms, particularly if two events occurred close together. (If they do not occur close together, such relationships might be trivial, as, for example, a finding that smiling onset regularly precedes language development.) Thirdly, we will look to see if there is a high degree of correlation among variables. If there is, it could point to cause-and-effect relationships or to common underlying mechanisms.

For convenience, we will consider questions about the EEG and behavior during two different periods, an early period and a later period.

An Early Period — New EEG Patterns and Their Relation to Fussing and Smiling

At approximately two to three months, sleep onset shifts from the postnatal pattern of beginning with active REM sleep to the subsequent childhood and adult pattern of beginning with quiet (NREM) sleep. In our initial longitudinal study, with biweekly EEGs, this shift was found to occur between three and nine weeks, the median age being seven weeks. The year-long study yielded similar findings. The age of shift to NREM sleep onset ranged from two to four months.[1]

Sleep spindles are known to develop during the first three

[1] It should be noted that the results of both studies are from infants falling asleep in our laboratory. Other research has indicated that the shift in sleep onset occurs later in the home environment, usually between three and five months, and that it is subject to more variation (Bernstein, Emde, and Campos, 1973; Kligman, Smyrl, and Emde, 1975). Perhaps the earlier age shift seen in the laboratory reflects a novelty or stress effect, similar to the "first-night effect" in adult sleep studies (Agnew, Webb, and Williams, 1966).

postnatal months (Metcalf, 1970; Lenard, 1970). On the basis of Metcalf's rating scale, two infants did not develop the mature form of spindles (Grade II) during the 14-week period of the initial longitudinal study. In those infants who did, onset ranged from nine to 13 weeks, the median being 11 weeks. All 12 infants developed an early form of spindles (Grade I) (range of onset, from five to 13 weeks; median, nine weeks). In the year-long study, onset of Grade I spindles ranged from one to three months and onset of Grade II spindles ranged from two to four months.

It would appear that this early period does represent a time of concentrated change in the development of the EEG. Table 3 illustrates the onset of these early patterns in the year-long study. In eight of the 14 infants in this study NREM sleep onset and Grade II spindles were first noted on the same EEG visit. In all other cases the two shifts occurred within a month of each other. In addition, these two EEG changes occurred at about the same time as two affective changes, namely, fussiness decline and smiling onset. The clustering of all these changes was in itself of considerable interest. Fortunately, our longitudinal design allowed us to look further, to see if there were regularities in sequences. In individual infants, for example, would affect behavior changes be consistently preceded by the EEG changes?

Except for one regularity, our results were negative. Neither rank order correlations nor binomial tests supported the hypothesis that the time of onset of social smiling was related

TABLE 3
ONSET OF EARLY SLEEP EEG PATTERNS

N = 14 Cases

	Age in Months											
	1	2	3	4	5	6	7	8	9	10	11	12
Sleep onset NREM	-	5	8	1	-	-	-	-	-	-	-	
Grade I Spindles	5	8	1	-	-	-	-	-	-	-	-	-
Grade II Spindles	-	8	5	1	-	-	-	-	-	-	-	-

to the time of onset of spindles or of NREM sleep onset. In a like manner, there was no support for the hypothesis that the decline of fussiness was related to the onset of sleep spindles. There was, however, evidence that fussiness decline tended to occur after the development of NREM sleep onset. (Fussiness decline was defined as a rating of less than 2 for at least two weeks; see Table B in Appendix.) In the initial study, NREM sleep onset preceded fussiness decline in 11 of 12 infants (binomial probability $p = < .01$); in the year-long study, 11 of 14 infants showed the same sequence (binomial probability $p = < .05$). As intriguing as this relationship seems, we must insert a note of caution about its interpretation. It is tempting to speculate that the developmental change in sleep onset has an organizing effect on the central nervous system and contributes to the decline of endogenous fussiness. But, as we have already mentioned, recent studies indicate that the shift in sleep onset occurs in the home environment at a later age than it does in the laboratory.[2]

A Later Period—New EEG Patterns and Their Relation to Stranger Distress and Separation Distress

Two additional EEG phenomena appear during the latter part of the first year: hypersynchronous drowsy activity and K-complexes. Like spindles, both patterns are absent at birth, appear during the first year, and continue throughout the life span. Hypersynchronous drowsy activity (HSD) has its maximal development between four and seven years, but makes its initial appearance at about three to five postnatal months (Metcalf, Mondale, and Butler, 1971). This activity is seen during the transition from wakefulness to sleep and consists of

[2] Rank order correlations were of little help in this analysis because of the large number of ties in each study. It is of interest, however, that in group data the distributions for time of onset of the two phenomena overlapped so completely that medians and ranges were practically identical.

high amplitude theta activity (4-8 Hz) with generalized synchrony. As in the case of spindles, we used a rating scale devised by Metcalf to score the maturation of this variable. A 2 rating was used to indicate onset. In 13 of our infants HSD developed between two and nine months. In the remaining infant, HSD did not appear during the first year. The median age of development for HSD was four months but the protracted range of onset of this pattern is more descriptive than its central tendency.

The second EEG phenomenon which has its onset during the latter part of the first year is the K-complex. This form of transient activity appears as a well-delineated negative sharp wave followed by a positive wave, usually most prominent in the vertex location of the scalp. When it appears in development, it is characteristic of NREM sleep thereafter. A 2 rating on Metcalf's K-complex scoring system was used as an indication of the onset of definitive though immature K-complexes. Onset occurred between four and nine months of age (median, six months). As with HSD onset, K-complex development was more scattered and had a greater range across individuals than did spindle development or NREM sleep onset. Table 4 displays the onset of these patterns.

TABLE 4
ONSET OF LATER SLEEP EEG PATTERNS

N = 14 Cases						Age in Months					
	1	2	3	4	5	6	7	8	9	10	11	12
HSD	0	1	0	7	2	0	1	1	1	0	0	0
K-Complexes	0	0	0	1	3	4	4	0	2	0	0	0

Examination of individual cases adds weight to the impression of a less concentrated time of onset for these two later EEG patterns. In only one infant did HSD and K-complexes initially appear during the same visit; in the other infants, their onset ranged from within one to five months of each other. Furthermore, there were no regularities in sequence between the two onset patterns: in nine of the infants HSD developed before the K-complex, and in four infants the reverse occurred. Nevertheless, it should be pointed out that there were no infants in whom either HSD or K-complexes appeared before the development of either Grade II spindles or NREM sleep onset.

Affect expressions which have their onset during the latter half of the first year are separation distress and stranger distress. As will be seen from our discussion in Chapter 10, the onset of stranger distress clustered around eight to nine months, and all of our infants developed it. The onset of separation distress, on the other hand, was more spread out and tended to occur later. Three of our longitudinal sample of 14 infants never developed separation distress during our period of study, and four others developed it only on the twelfth month's visit. Because the onset of separation distress was so much later than the onset of the EEG variables, statistics about regularities in sequences are of little interest. We do think it important, however, that the rank order correlations between separation distress and the EEG variables were low and therefore give no basis for postulating causal links or common underlying mechanisms.

The onset of stranger distress is of more interest to us since it clustered in closer proximity to the developmental changes seen in the EEG. These tended to develop before stranger distress, but since there were exceptions, we must reject the hypothesis of any necessary sequences. Eleven of the 14 infants developed K-complexes before stranger distress (binomial probability $p = < .05$) and 12 of the 14 developed HSD before stranger distress ($p = < .05$). The HSD relationship, however, may be misleading since the median for the onset of this variable (four months) is still far removed from that of stranger distress (eight months). Rank order correlations between the EEG variables and stranger distress were, once again, low, suggesting that one should be cautious in speculating about common factors.

The EEG and Other Behavioral Changes

The onset of these EEG changes was also compared with our rated categories of illness, feeding changes, and stress events (see Chapter 12). We believed that there were a number of possibilities for relationships between the EEG changes and these other events, based either on primary changes in the central nervous system leading to a vulnerability, or on major experiential changes affecting the EEG (such as Metcalf's [1969] demonstration of the impact of experience on accelerating development of sleep spindles). With one exception, no clear relationships were found, either by rank order correlations or by inspection of individual cases. The exception was suggested by one infant in whom there was a rather striking correspondence between a move to an unfamiliar bedroom and a change in the onset of her sleep. Her NREM sleep onset at two months was the earliest exhibited by any of our infants. As previously mentioned, there are now data from two other studies indicating that environmental stress may result in an earlier NREM sleep onset pattern (Bernstein, Emde, and Campos, 1973; Kligman, Smyrl, and Emde, 1975).

Conclusion: Clustering of Changes but No Invariant Sequences

In answer to the questions raised at the beginning of this chapter, we concluded the following. There does appear to be a clustering of developmental changes seen in the EEG during the first year. This is most concentrated during an earlier period (two to three months for spindles and sleep onset shift) and less concentrated during a later period (four to seven months in most cases for HSD and K-complex onset). Evidence for regularities in sequences between these changes and major changes in affect expressions is weak. There are no invariant sequences between sectors, although some EEG changes tend to occur before some affect behavior changes. Rank order correlations between the onset of EEG patterns and changes in affect behaviors were all low. These negative findings are important data for any speculations concerning antecedent-consequent relationships or common underlying mechanisms.

PART III

THE DEVELOPMENT OF
EMOTIONAL EXPRESSIONS

6

THE EARLY POSTNATAL PERIOD: UNEXPLAINED SMILING

According to the genetic field theory the social smile, which normally makes its regular appearance at around two and a half months, is the first indicator of a time of rapid change. Very early in our research we became convinced of the need to study antecedents of social smiling. Theoretical discussions of such smiling often rested on the assumption that it appeared suddenly and without precursors. Our initial observations indicated otherwise. During the early weeks we saw facial expressions which often puzzled us—a bilateral upturning of the corners of the mouth occurring sporadically in a variety of behavioral states. Mothers tended to make light of these early smiles and to ignore them; they referred to some of them as "gas expressions" and to others as "smiling at the angels." Köhler (1954) and Wolff (1959) described newborn smiles during sleep and drowsiness, and there are other descriptions of early smiles during wakefulness (Wolff, 1963, 1966). However, we realized there was an urgent need for further systematic study of early smiling and its correlates. If smiling had precursors which began at birth, if it had a gradual onset, there might be less evidence for the rapid change postulated in the genetic field theory. These considerations led us on a quest which eventuated in a number of cross-sectional and short-term studies.

As a result, our vision broadened. In this chapter we will describe two systems of smiling which arise in development before the predictable social smiling response. One system arises from the inside as a correlate of an observed behavioral and physiological state pattern. For that reason, we decided to refer to it as *endogenous.* The other system is stimulated from the outside, and we refer to it as *exogenous*. Unlike the other chapters of this monograph, much of the work described here has been published previously, and therefore much will be summarized. The interested reader is referred to the earlier publications cited in the text below for details of rationale, data, and statistical analysis.

Early Endogenous Smiling

This form of smiling is not the result of external stimulation. It occurs "spontaneously," as a manifestation of endogenously determined physiological rhythms during the REM state. As such, it appears to be one of many circumscribed state-related behaviors which occur shortly after birth. Several studies led us to the conclusion that endogenous smiling is a consistent correlate of the REM state (Emde and Koenig, 1969a, 1969b; Emde and Metcalf, 1970).

The reader may wonder why, in this context, we use the phrase "REM state" instead of "REM sleep." A surprising finding was that endogenous smiling occurs not only during REM sleep when the eyes are closed, but also at times when there are behavioral activity patterns and polygraphic patterns of REM-sleep with eyes open. We decided to call this state, which appeared to be a behavioral form of drowsiness, "drowsy REM." The discovery of what some might consider to be a "nonsleep" REM state was soon enlarged to include other behavioral states. Although they were not correlated with smiling, *nutritional sucking, fussing,* and *crying* exhibited the common electrophysiology of the "REM state" during certain times of the feeding cycle. This electrophysiology included: eye movements, a relatively desynchronized mixed-frequency EEG, irregular respirations, and suppressed muscle tone when measured from the chin. Because a variety of apparent behavioral states shared this electrophysiology and because these states tended to disappear during the early months, we referred to them as the "behaviorally undifferentiated REM states" of early infancy. Much research remains to be done concerning reactivity during these states.

As we collected more and more data, we found that endogenous smiling is a consistent correlate of sleep REM and drowsy REM. There was no evidence that this smiling was related to "gas," as was suggested by folklore. It was found to occur during the REM state with an average density of 11 smiles per hundred minutes of observed state no matter where the observation was made in the feeding cycle or the 24-hour cycle. There was also a tendency for it to occur in bursts. More than a third of the smiles in full-term newborns were observed during the same minute as another smile. This tendency to cluster was supported by two different statistical tests. Another study documented a tendency for endogenous smiling to be correlated with an expectable electrophysiological pattern within the REM state.

The tendency of endogenous smiling to occur at the same average rate across REM periods was not paralleled in the case of endogenous frowning. Spontaneous frowning also had a base rate during REM periods, but it increased beyond base rates during final REM periods before the infant awoke, cried, and was fed. Thus, during sleep, frowning appeared to be both a spontaneous REM-state behavior and also a potential indicator of hunger distress and/or impending awakening. Endogenous smiling carried with it no such additional indications.

We wondered if this form of smiling might be mediated by structures in the limbic system. This hypothesis seemed plausible, since there is evidence of limbic activation in adult REM sleep and since the limbic system has been thought of as the highest level of integration for emotional expression. However, subsequent data that we collected made this formulation doubtful. First, in a study of premature infants, we found a great deal more REM smiling in them than in full-term infants (Emde, McCartney, and Harmon, 1971). Figure 5 illustrates a negative correlation between the density of smiling and postconceptional age (rho = -.71). This seemed particularly damaging to our hypothesis about limbic mediation, since limbic structures in the premature, even at eight months gestational age, are considerably less mature

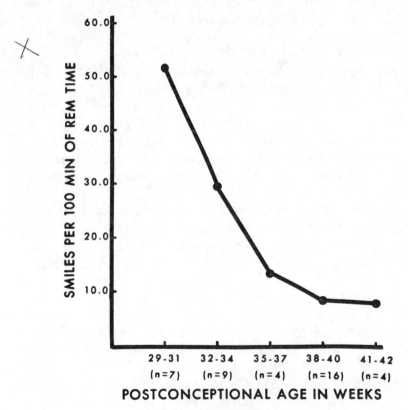

FIGURE 5

than limbic structures in the full-term newborn (Rabinowicz, 1964).

An additional opportunity to test the limbic mediation hypothesis arose when we had the opportunity to make behavioral and subsequent neuroanatomical observations of a newborn with severe microcephalus (Harmon and Emde, 1972). We observed this infant, with a clinical diagnosis of congenital toxoplasmosis, for one month after she was born. She died just before her second month's birthday, after a paralytic ileus. Neuroanatomical examination supported the inference that, during the time we observed her, there was severe impairment of both the cerebral cortex and limbic system while the brain stem was relatively intact. Both cerebral hemispheres were markedly calcified and the brain weight was nearly one tenth of what is expectable at that age. But the most dramatic aspects of this case were the behavioral correlations. During life, not only did this infant show cyclical alternations of REM and NREM, of activity and quiescence; she also manifested endogenous smiling and other spontaneous REM behaviors at rates which were consistently within one standard deviation of mean values for a normal full-term comparison group matched for postconceptional age.

As a result of the microcephalic and premature infant studies, we arrived at the following view of endogenous smiling. It is probably organized and mediated within the brain stem along with frowning, mouth movements, and other REM-related spontaneous behaviors which also occurred at characteristic "normal" rates in our microcephalic case. As a result of increasing neurological inhibition, probably related to maturation of the cerebral cortex, endogenous smiling diminishes during the early months of infancy. Preliminary longitudinal observations indicate that this form of smiling normally diminishes during the third and fourth postnatal months but continues into the fifth or sixth month, thereafter becoming a rarity. Current research is aimed at systematically describing the frequency of these behaviors beyond the newborn period.

EARLY EXOGENOUS SMILING

Unlike endogenous smiling, the exogenous smiling system is not present at birth. It begins in an irregular fashion during the first or second month, and increases in specificity and importance throughout the first year, and indeed throughout the life span. Our studies have shown that during the period when it is irregular, from one and a half to two and a half months, visual, kinesthetic, auditory, and tactile stimuli will elicit it. We might think of this age as one during which there is nonspecific smiling, or smiling in response to multiple stimuli. There is a flowering of the response, the infant smiling in response to "everything," but it is not predictable (Emde and Harmon, 1972). After this, from two and a half to three months, the regular social smile occurs. Now smiling is best elicited by visual stimuli, especially the human face, although it increases in response to stimuli in other modalities as well. During the next phase, at three months and after, there is early differentiated smiling. Smiling becomes more specific within the visual modality, requiring a three-dimensional stimulus configuration, and soon there is more smiling in response to the mother's face than to others. Concomitantly, smiling becomes rare in response to nonvisual stimuli.

The data seem consistent with the viewpoint that there is a maturational "push," a time in development when there is a propensity to smile at everything. For a brief period, a wide variety of moderately intense stimuli will elicit smiling. After three months of age, nonspecific smiling does not survive, presumably because, unlike social smiling, it is not normally reinforced in the infant's social context. Thus, maturation would seem to be the major determinant of the onset of smiling in response to multiple stimuli, while learning would account for its subsequent shaping and inhibition. This viewpoint receives striking support from observations of congenitally blind infants (Fraiberg, 1971). Although without vision from birth, these infants exhibit the same early phases of smiling in response to multiple stimuli; this phase is followed by one of specific smiling, but with shaping to an auditory-tactile gestalt rather than to a visual one.

Another surprising finding was that, during the earlier period when there was smiling at "everything," there was often smiling and frowning in response to the same relatively brief stimulus presentation. It was as if there were some kind of response equivalence for smiling. Werner's (1948) theory, which describes undifferentiated phases of development in terms of a tendency for systems to function in a global manner, was used to explain these equivalences (Emde and Harmon, 1972).

RELATIONSHIPS BETWEEN EARLY SMILING SYSTEMS

We then wondered if the two systems of early smiling were related. One type of smiling occurred during sleep and drowsy REM states and the other type occurred during wakefulness. One required stimulation and the other did not. We assumed that two different maturational systems were using elements of the same motor pathway. Since they overlapped temporally, we thought that they should also interact. Werner's developmental theory seemed to suggest that there might be an overflow of activation between undifferentiated systems with some kind of summation effect. On this basis, we predicted that an experimental state with enhanced smiling could be induced during the period of overlap. We gently awakened one- to two-months-old babies from sleep in order to achieve various degrees of drowsiness so that we could stimulate them. By this means, we believe we discovered an intermediate phenomenon between the two systems of smiling. A mild amount of nonspecific stimulation (such as ringing a bell, turning the infant over, picking him up, rocking him) aroused infants to a drowsy state and elicited continual repetitive smiling of a sustained frequency greater than that of either endogenous or exogenous smiling. Sometimes an initial stimulus was enough to set off repetitive smiling for 10 minutes or more. On other occasions, intermittent low-level stimulation, such as rocking or jiggling, was necessary to keep the infant in the aroused drowsy state with repetitive smiling. Following this period, infants would either drift back into REM sleep or awaken. The repetitive smiles we set in motion averaged 1.5 per minute—a density over 15 times that of spontaneous smiling in full-term infants during sleep and drowsy REM! In a typical case, 16 repetitive smiles were generated in this manner. The smiles were not clustered around a few burst minutes like REM smiles. The further developmental description of such smiles, as well as the electrophysiological correlates of the aroused drowsy state, are matters for future research.

Conclusion: A Shift from Endogenous to Exogenous control

From these studies, we concluded that the period from two and one half to three months is a nodal one in the development of smiling. Smiling undergoes a major shift from "unexplained smiling" to smiling with social meaning. There is a shift from endogenous to exogenous control, and then the response system becomes more complex. Exogenous smiling is preceded by a diminution in the number of external stimuli that will automatically elicit it, and is followed by an expansion in the number of complex internal cognitive and other factors which may be predisposing determinants. After this time, the commonly used physiological states of the neonatal period (Hutt, Lenard, and Prechtl, 1969; Anders, Emde, and Parmelee, 1971) no longer suffice as useful descriptions of an organismic readiness to smile. Instead, "moods" are of increasing importance in determining such readiness. Such "moods" receive contributions not only from physiological processes but also from expanding psychological processes of memory, cognition, and need representations.

7

THE EARLY POSTNATAL PERIOD: UNEXPLAINED FUSSINESS

Besides early smiling, there is another early affect expression which often puzzles mothers. All babies cry when hungry or in response to pain, but unexplainable crying also occurs. This form of crying, usually referred to as "fussiness," causes bewilderment even in experienced mothers. They often find their infants difficult to soothe, and express uneasiness about their failure. Occasionally they try to ignore the fussiness, and console themselves with the thought that the baby will outgrow it. This fussiness appears to be equally puzzling to researchers. Previous studies of it have concentrated on extreme instances which come to the attention of pediatricians and are often labeled "infantile colic" (Stewart et al., 1954; Wessel et al., 1954; Brazelton, 1962; Paradise, 1966). In our longitudinal studies we took a different approach. We followed normal infants in an attempt to focus on all instances of unexplained fussiness, not just extreme cases. About one-fourth of the infants we studied developed extreme fussiness; some were in fact unofficially labeled as having "colic" by pediatricians. However, one of our major findings was that significant periods of unexplained fussiness occurred during early infancy in *all* the infants we studied. Furthermore, such fussiness appeared to have a typical developmental course which was largely independent of variations in mothering.

We concerned ourselves with fussing and crying which were not clearly related to physiological need or specific externally caused discomfort. In both our longitudinal studies, fussiness was rated from typed transcripts of mothers' reports of fussiness and other behaviors which had occurred since the time of the last visit (two-week intervals in the first study; four-week intervals in the second study). Whenever fussing occurred during home visits we paid particular attention to it and compared our observations with the mothers' descriptions of it. Our definition of fussiness and rating criteria can be found in Table B (see Appendix).

INITIAL LONGITUDINAL STUDY

The first study was designed to test certain ideas of John Benjamin's concerning fussiness and its correlates during the first three months of life. The results of this study supported Benjamin's (1965) predictions about the developmental course of early fussiness. He predicted a period of increased fussiness at three to four weeks and a decline at eight to 10 weeks of age. Table 5 shows the fussiness ratings from this longitudinal study. The significance of the difference between means comparing each week with every other week is consistent with an initial increase followed by a plateau. (Using a t test, ratings for weeks two through nine are significantly higher than the rating for the first week, with significance beyond the .01 level; week four is significantly higher than week 13.) As the standard deviations indicate, at nine weeks and beyond between-subject variability increases. An analysis of our data showed that in the tenth week the distribution of fussiness was bimodal: the three fussiest infants were still given high ratings, whereas the fussiness of other infants had markedly declined.

Those aspects of this study that addressed Benjamin's formulations concerning an active and passive stimulus barrier

TABLE 5

MEAN VALUES OF FUSSINESS RATINGS BY WEEKLY INTERVALS:
INITIAL LONGITUDINAL STUDY

WEEKS

	1	2	3	4	5	6	7	8	9	10	11	12	13
Mean Rating	.17	.86	1.62	1.81	1.59	1.55	1.55	1.58	1.54	1.58	1.71	1.39	1.15
s.d.	.30	.82	.96	.79	.70	.84	.91	.75	1.13	1.36	1.50	1.09	.94
N	10	12	12	12	12	12	12	12	12	12	12	10	10

are the subject of another report (Tennes et al., 1972). Suffice it to say that we did not find any evidence of a dramatically emerging new capacity to avoid stimulation (active stimulus barrier) associated with the decline in fussiness. Instead, we found evidence of a new stimulus facilitation system emerging during this time, namely, the smiling response. Only later did motor capacities to turn away and attention-diverting capacities become prominent.

LONGITUDINAL STUDY OF THE FIRST YEAR

The fussiness findings in our second longitudinal study appear to replicate those of the initial study: there exists a period of prolonged nonhunger fussiness which is most common during the first three months of life. Although fussiness wanes at three months, it does not reach a negligible point, on the average, until six months.

Figure 6 illustrates the mean curve for fussiness throughout the first year of life. It illustrates that nothing quite like the fussiness of the first six months was found in the second half of the first year. The mean curve, however, is somewhat misleading in that it is composed of three relatively distinct temporal patterns. The patterns are schematically represented in Figure 7. Pattern A, an *early pattern,* consists of maximal fussiness from one to three months with a sharp decline afterwards (N = 6). Pattern B, an *intermediate pattern,* consists of maximal fussiness from two to five months with a sharp decline afterwards (N = 5). Pattern C, a *prolonged pattern,* consists of intense fussiness between one and four months with a long slow decline from four to seven months (N = 3). The existence of these three patterns, although seen in a sample of only 14 infants, may be of more general interest. In fact, they may partly account for differences between the mean values of fussiness in the first study and in the second study. The increase in variability after nine weeks found in the first study could well have been a reflection of the emergence of one of the later patterns whose total effect was not realized since the study ended at 14 weeks.

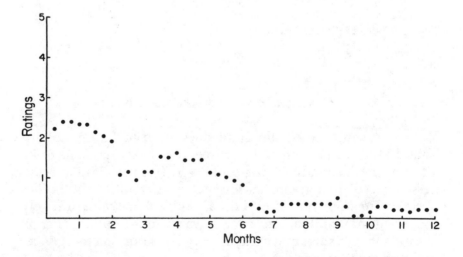

FIGURE 6. Mean curve of fussiness. All 14 cases are represented at each data point.

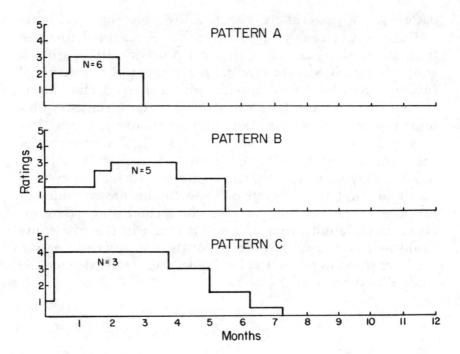

FIGURE 7. Schematic representation of three temporal patterns
of prolonged fussiness.

CONCLUSION: AN EARLY ENDOGENOUS FUSSINESS

Early fussiness is puzzling and does seem to be unexplainable. In the period from one to three months there seems to be
an endogenous readiness for prolonged fussiness. Since fussiness occurred to a greater or lesser degree in all of the babies
observed in both our longitudinal studies, it seems unlikely
that environmental factors, such as variations in mothering or
changes in the surround, play a major role in its emergence,
maintenance, or decline.

Since there appears to us to be an inborn readiness for
prolonged nonhunger fussiness, we have wondered about its

evolutionary purpose. Bowlby (1969) has made a strong case for the central role of crying in ensuring early infant-mother attachment—a function crucial for survival in the human species. We agree with this view. Crying gives a peremptory message to the mother: "Come close; change what is happening, if possible." One could imagine that a tendency toward prolonged fussiness was built into the human infant to ensure survival by promoting closeness with a caretaker at times *not* necessarily taken up with feeding.

8

SOCIAL SMILING AND
A NEW LEVEL OF ORGANIZATION

When the young infant begins to smile regularly in response
to the moving face of another, his social life takes a leap
forward. His mother, father, and other family members are
delighted by his beaming response. He is shown off to friends
of the family who no longer feel they always have to tiptoe in
the house of a sleeping baby. Instead, he smiles engagingly at
everyone, his eyes brightly fixated on those of the person who
looks at him. About two weeks after the regular social smile
makes its appearance, he adds a cooing vocalization as
another specific accompaniment of the social encounter. His
mother automatically experiences delight and a feeling that
her infant is delighted. An often heard comment, especially by
parents of a first-born, is that now they feel that their baby is
human; before, he was more of a doll-like object to be
protected and taken care of.

THE CHANGED MEANING OF SMILING AT
TWO AND A HALF MONTHS AND AFTER

An analysis of what is communicated by the young infant's
affect expressions is most illuminating. From what we have
observed in the homes of our longitudinally studied infants,
we agree completely with the previous conclusions of Ambrose

(1963) and Stechler and Carpenter (1967). Crying, the predominant affective behavior of the first two months, gives a universal and peremptory message to the caretaker. It communicates: "Come, change what's happening." Ordinarily the caretaker responds by soothing the infant, either specifically by feeding, changing a diaper, changing a position, or nonspecifically by rocking, stroking, or holding. During times of unexplained crying, when a mother cannot soothe her infant, we can see how frustrating it is for her: the built-in communication system has gone awry, and she does not get the necessary feedback from her infant's being soothed. She often continues a variety of soothing techniques in exasperation, and if the frustration cycle continues, she may become alarmed and consult a pediatrician.

No such vicious cycle results from unexplained smiling. Smiling also gives a universal message, but it is not an urgent request for change. It communicates, "Keep up what you are doing. I like it." Furthermore, mothers like it. The message of the smile is not peremptory; it is not an immediate call to action. Thus mothers can easily ignore the smiling that occurs during REM sleep when the infant's eyes are closed. Although they are puzzled by the irregular smiling during wakefulness which occurs in response to a wide variety of nonsocial stimuli, they do not experience frustration. Some mothers, when interviewed in detail, may show signs of being mildly hurt that their baby is not smiling more at them as compared with the lamp or the bookcase, but it is generally in the context of some amusement, along with the hopeful anticipation that the baby will soon "wise up" and smile mostly at them.

As we discussed in Chapter 6, it is soon after the period of smiling at "everything" that smiling becomes more specifically social. In contrast to earlier smiling—both endogenous and exogenous—social smiling can now be influenced by the mother's behavior. That the infant's social smiling and cooing are subject to shaping by operant conditioning was demonstrated experimentally in the often quoted studies of Brackbill

(1958) and Rheingold, Gewirtz, and Ross (1959). Equally true, but perhaps more important, is the fact that mothers derive enormous enjoyment from making their babies smile. In other words, mothers' behaviors are now positively reinforced and shaped by their infants' smiling. This aspect of social smiling has not been studied at all, but it would seem to deserve a systematic, naturalistic study in the future.

A New Level of Organization: Using Wakefulness Differently

The dramatic shift from virtually no exogenous smiling to a surge of nonspecific smiling before smiling becomes specifically social, the fact of the flowering itself, seems to argue for a strong maturational thrust in smiling onset. It is as if a shift in the organism's state of readiness, in CNS organization, must take place before smiling appears. Thereafter, learning is increasingly influential, and smiling becomes modified; it becomes adapted to a specific environment. This view supplements cognitive theories which account for infant smiling in terms of a developing ability to recognize familiar objects (Piaget, 1936; Zelazo and Komer, 1971; Zelazo, 1972; Kagan, 1970, 1971). At its onset, there is smiling in response to a wide variety of stimuli, *unfamiliar as well as familiar;* thus a shift in maturational readiness may primarily account for the early manifestations of exogenous smiling. This view about maturation led us to suspect a new level of biobehavioral organization following this shift. Let us review other evidence.

Although the infant's total amount of wakefulness does not increase with the onset of social smiling (see Figure 1, Chapter 1), he appears to begin using his periods of wakefulness differently. Not only does he smile, coo, and engage other humans around him in a variety of stimulus-maintaining social behaviors, he also shows a dramatic change in his interaction with his nonhuman surroundings. Beginning at this time, there is an ever-increasing curiosity, an interest in the novel, and, eventually, a surge in exploratory activities. The beginning of this period is marked by a decline in unexplained fussing, as indicated by our data and data from a number of other studies (Brazelton, 1962; Dittrichova and Lapackova, 1964). The infant soon enters a stage of cognitive development which Piaget (1936) labeled as the time of engaging in "procedures designed to make interesting spectacles last." One can be impressed by the fact that the infant before two months communicates so as to change and often reduce stimulation by crying. On the other hand, the infant after two months has a new system of communication, namely smiling, which is potentially stimulus facilitating. He now has many other behaviors with which he actively engages the world; he increases the level and variety of stimulus input rather than seeking to reduce it. The notion of a fundamental change in wakefulness during this time was originally suggested by Kleitman (1939) and given substance by Dittrichova and Lapackova (1964) in their longitudinal studies from the Institute of the Care of the Mother and Child in Prague. They studied infants at weekly intervals from two to 24 weeks and concluded: "Taking in conjunction the findings with regard to toy manipulation, babbling, and crying, it seems apparent that in the second and third month significant changes occur in the development of the waking state in infants; manipulation in play and babbling increase, and crying decreases. These findings . . . suggest that functional changes in the central nervous system take place, the nature of which require further study" (pp. 369-370).

This is quite different from the under-two-months infant, whose behavioral organization often seems to fit the "discharge" or hydraulic model. Some recent research findings are illustrative. In the newborn it seems that one can affect the *distribution* of behavioral states but one cannot change their *total amount* by interventions such as feeding schedules (Gaensbauer and Emde, 1973) or awakening manipulations

(Anders and Roffwarg, 1973). In addition, there is evidence that spontaneous sleep behaviors, such as smiles, erections, and startles, can be thought of summatively—one behavior may substitute for another (Wolff, 1960; Korner, 1969). That a similar situation may obtain for eye-movement patterns in waking visual fixations in early infancy is indicated by recent work of Daniel Stern (personal communication). Thus it appears that a great deal of the behavioral repertoire at this early age is of a fixed amount and under homeostatic regulation; any deficit incurred at one time moves toward a compensated extra amount at a later time, and any surplus is counterbalanced by a later deficit.

This situation is in striking contrast to the predominant behavioral organization after the onset of the social smile. Now there is a considerable increase in stimulus-maintaining and stimulus-seeking activity. It seems as if there is a surge of growing and metabolizing, with a new capacity for gaining increasing amounts of energy from the environment for use in psychological differentiation and structure building. The infant seeks "nutriments" and new experience. On another level of abstraction, this is a very different state of affairs from that of the newborn, who often, though not exclusively, behaves according to what Spitz (1959) described as the "nirvana" or "pain-quiescence principle."

A HUMAN REBIRTH? SOME EVOLUTIONARY CONSIDERATIONS

Is there some evolutionary significance in this fundamental shift in the behavioral economy of the young infant? As we watched the development of the babies in our study through this time, we were consistently impressed by its dramatic qualities. It seemed like a new awakening. Taking a lead from the feelings expressed by many of the parents in our study, we often imagined this shift as a "human rebirth."

We were reminded of the proposal put forth by the cultural

anthropologist, Ashley Montagu, over a decade ago (1961), that the human infant is born two to three months too soon. The relatively early birth was occasioned in evolution, he reasoned, as a consequence of man's upright posture, which led to greater specialization of the hands, a diminished jaw, and a larger cranial cavity; these changes occurred at the same time that the pelvic outlet became narrower owing to the same upright posture. The result was, of course, a cephalopelvic disproportion, necessitating an earlier passage through the birth canal for the survival of both mother and infant. This, reasoned Montagu, resulted in the human infant's extended state of "neotany" or helplessness, with immature systems requiring the total care of the mother. We now know that this explanation cannot hold in any strict way for the human being. The cat, which did not evolve to an erect posture, is also born helpless, and, on the level of neurophysiology, its postnatal shift is strikingly similar to the human's (see Chapter 1). But perhaps there is adaptive value in such a shift in itself. Perhaps we can learn more from a functional analysis of adaptation in the human and other species without regard to evolutionary lines of ancestry. Thinking in this manner, could there be adaptive value in the postnatal change as we have described it? Certain facts about crying and smiling are especially intriguing.

Crying is predominant as a social response after birth. It declines afterward, but not because of the mother's lack of attention to it (see discussion in Bell and Ainsworth, 1972). Instead, crying seems to decline according to an internal program; with development, other responses (and signals) take its place. One would assume that this shift reflects a maturational timetable, one fashioned as a result of evolution.

Smiling reflects a different timetable. It is not predominant as a social response immediately after birth. But, as we have discussed, the way in which it gains ascendancy makes us again think of the major influence of maturation. Our question now becomes somewhat more focused: What could be the adaptive value of such a timetable? Why should one affect expression decline and the other rise?

We speculate that crying gained pre-eminence in evolution because of its obvious importance as a peremptory social signal, one necessary for the survival of the helpless infant. Smiling, on the other hand, has different attributes. It did not emerge as immediately necessary for survival; even more to the point, its message for stimulus maintenance and/or enhancement might be maladaptive in the newborn. It could produce a stimulus "overload" which would disrupt an already delicate balance of vital functions. Furthermore, from an interactive point of view, social smiling, if it occurred in the newborn, could promote a false sense of security in the caretaker. Only later, when physiological stability is assured, is social smiling adaptive. Its value then includes both enhancing the mother's good feelings about her baby and ensuring an increasing variety of social and nonsocial stimulation at a time when the quality of wakefulness seems to shift and can be used in a new way.

Again, the question of animal models is important. If such speculation is useful, we should be able to find analogies in other species, situations where similar lines of functional adaptation have occurred. Once having done this, experimentation is possible and the scientific search for basic mechanisms can proceed. In Chapter 1, the cat emerged as a possible animal model for an early biobehavioral shift. It occurs to us that this model may also include variables analogous to human "affect expressions." The newborn kitten, like the newborn human, has a distress vocalization-quiescence organization; purring has its onset only later, perhaps during the very time of the neurophysiological shift being studied by Chase (1973) and McGinty (1971). We are also struck by the situation in the dog, in which a similar functional adaptation may have occurred. Like many species, the dog also has a distress vocalization immediately after birth. However, as Scott (1963) has so nicely documented, it is only after three weeks that tail-wagging has its onset. At the very least, it seems that the existence of such "affective" shifts in the infancy of other mammals offers major grounds for further research.

9

AN INTERVENING PERIOD: THE QUESTION OF SOCIAL DISCRIMINATION WITHOUT DISTRESS

In some earlier research, we found that soon after regular social smiling starts, a baby becomes more particular about what makes him smile (Polak, Emde, and Spitz, 1964b; Emde and Koenig, 1969b). By three months, he usually smiles less at a two-dimensional than at a three-dimensional visual representation of the face. At four months, he generally smiles less at unfamiliar people than at his mother. In congenitally blind infants, there is evidence to suggest that selective smiling in response to the mother's voice occurs at an earlier age (Freedman, 1965; Fraiberg, 1971). In other terms, the four-month-old baby can show us that in some sense he "knows" his mother as compared with someone strange. He is more responsive to her and seems more delighted by her. But the four-month-old baby does not avoid the stranger or protest his approach with a cry. His discrimination between mother and stranger is indicated by a relative absence of smiling (and often by an absence of cooing and bodily excitement), not by the presence of distress behavior. Crying, the first affect expression in the infant's repertoire, is not yet incorporated into this strictly social context. It is as if crying were still a signal governed more by physiological than by psychological upset.

94

In planning our longitudinal study, we wondered about this situation. Why should crying at the sight of a stranger appear only later? Why not at four months? A number of studies have shown that such crying typically does not emerge for another three or four months (Tennes and Lampl, 1964; Schaffer and Emerson, 1964; Morgan and Ricciuti, 1969). Why should there be such a time lag between social discrimination and social distress? It would be consistent with the genetic field theory to think of the age period of four to seven months as one of a slower rate of change, of consolidation. But we wondered further: Did increased cognitive discrimination await a later CNS maturational event before stranger distress could appear? If such an event occurred, we postulated that we would see evidence of a rapid integration of the new system soon afterward.

As we began our work, we realized that this formulation implied the sudden appearance of distress in response to a stranger without affect expressions which could be thought of as developmental precursors. This notion was bolstered by previous studies in which stranger distress was found to develop abruptly and reach peak intensity soon after onset (Schaffer and Emerson, 1964; Tennes and Lampl, 1964). But were we justified in simply assuming this to be so? We thought not. Because of these considerations, we designed our filmed social-interaction series to detect early signs of stranger distress or its possible antecedents from four months on. But before presenting these results, it is instructive to review what we learned from our mothers about when they thought social discrimination began.

Social Discrimination from Interview Data

In our monthly interviews, we included the following open-ended inquiry: "Do you feel your infant knows you, and if so, in what way?" At the one-month visit, four of the 14 mothers in our longitudinal study answered that their infants "recognized" them by virtue of *easier soothability and/or easier feeding*. Father, grandmother, neighbor were not responded to in the same way. At the two-months visit, four more mothers answered our inquiry in a similar fashion. Two more spoke of such differential responsiveness at three months; four mothers never answered us in this way. We infer that soothability and feeding responsiveness contain less certain information about this matter than does another category of responses which mothers volunteered, namely that of *smiling, cooing, and general bodily activity*. Here, all mothers were convinced that their infants gave clear messages about when they knew their mothers from other adults. Mothers had an easy sense of the social meaning of this kind of response. According to our interview findings, none of our mothers thought that their infants could differentiate them in this way at one month; five did at two months. By three months 11 and by four months 13 mothers spoke of such differential responses. By five months, all 14 mothers were certain that their infants smiled, cooed, or showed a different kind of excited motor response to them.

What does this mean? In evaluating this kind of evidence, we soon realized that mothers were interpreting the development of an adaptive transaction. Changes were taking place in mothers *and* infants — changes which Sander (1962, 1964) describes in his studies of mother-infant interaction as "negotiations" toward new "reciprocal coordinations." Our first designated category of "soothability and feeding responsiveness" is one in which such negotiations were likely to be somewhat lopsided, the mother adapting more than the infant. The situation can be described as one in which the infant, with only a limited behavioral repertoire, is adapting to a mother who has at her disposal a wide range of behaviors which she can use in learning to "tune in." Even though the newborn modulates basic activities such as sucking and maintenance of posture, a large amount of the differential responsiveness reported by mothers during the first two postnatal months was probably a result of their learning to match their own responses to their particular infants. Our second category of responsiveness seems to be of a different nature. Smiling and cooing involve distance receptors, both visual and auditory, and seem more dependent on the infant's progressively learned discriminations. Less maternal adaptation is required.

SOCIAL DISCRIMINATION FROM FILMED INTERACTION SERIES

Our filmed interaction series provided us with a way of looking at the discriminating infant through our own eyes rather than through the mother's eyes. It also provided an opportunity for repeated viewing of a standardized experimental sequence so that we could establish interjudge reliability and reliability over time (see Chapter 3).

The films revealed that the infant of four to six months shows an intense interest in the stranger; when his mother returns, he very often looks longer at the stranger. This response of looking longer at a stranger than at a familiar person will come as no surprise to those familiar with the literature on "orienting" (see Bronshtein and Petrova, 1952; Graham and Clifton, 1966) and the literature on the tendency of the infant to attend to novel or moderately discrepant stimuli (see, for example, Hunt, 1965, and Kagan, 1971). In addition to looking longer at the stranger, the infant often made a visual comparison of his face with the mother's. A typical response was: looking at the mother's face, then at the stranger's face, and then back at the mother's, this sequence sometimes being repeated several times. In our categorized response of "compares faces," we required that a minimum sequence involve at least two looks at the stranger's face and one look at the mother's. This sequence occurred in all babies and its onset showed a developmental concentration: all infants had developed the response by five months, 13 of 14 having developed it either during the fourth or fifth month's visit. Once it appeared, the response characteristically continued for two or more months and then declined.

We thought that comparing faces reflected some kind of internal cognitive matching process. During the first month or two of its appearance, the infant's facial expression accompanying this behavior seemed to communicate interest; it seemed like a manifestation of problem-solving rather than pleasure. Later a fascinated look seemed colored with an uncertain, negative quality, which often became a "sober expression." To our surprise, film ratings of "sobering" illustrated a definite developmental onset before the intense frowning, fussing, and crying of stranger distress. The onset of sobering was concentrated in the five to seven months period. Although its onset was more spread out than that of comparing faces, it showed a clear developmental curve which preceded the onset of stranger distress by one to two months.

Figure 8 shows the relationship of the onset of the three responses of: compares faces, sober expression, and stranger distress. Data is from the first stranger approach of our social-

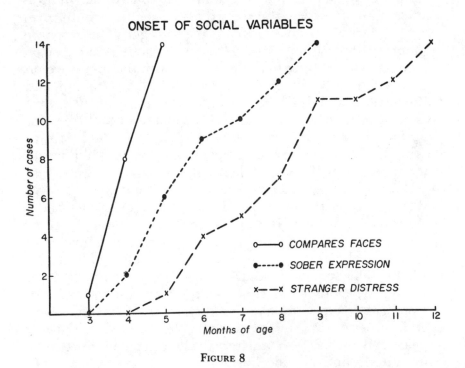

FIGURE 8

interaction series. The stranger distress measure used in this figure is our global impression of pronounced frowning, fussing, or crying.

These data indicate that stranger distress, like the regular social smile, has predictable behavioral antecedents. As was the case in our research on early smiling, we found evidence of an affective response which preceded the more intense response but did not convey the same dramatic and unambiguous message. The data on sobering add a new dimension to the question posed at the beginning of this chapter. The onset of stranger distress is not totally abrupt. Sobering in response to a stranger appears to be an expectable developmental event, generally preceding overt stranger distress by one or two months.

The Development of Recognition in Piaget's Sensorimotor Theory

Jean Piaget's sensorimotor theory is now the subject of much discussion and experimental study. It is attractive not only because of its explanatory power and logical consistency, but also because it is a view of the infant's expanding cognitive world based on clearly defined observations. It is important to discuss it here because it deals with the infant's increasing capacity to recognize the familiar. The six stages of sensorimotor development span the time from birth to about 18 months. The first two stages conceptualize an early form of recognition and shed light on our social discrimination data from maternal interviews. The second two stages, sensorimotor stages three and four, deal with the period under discussion in this chapter, a time during which, as Piaget's research has shown us, an infant may not know that a person continues to exist once he is out of his sight. Stages five and six will be reviewed because they illustrate the infant's progressive development toward evocative memory.

A. EARLY RECOGNITION

In Piaget's system of cognitive development, the infant, soon after birth, learns to "recognize" certain aspects of his environment by virtue of his prior action in accommodating to them. A recognitory act, in this sense, can be thought of as inherent in the infant's motor response to a familiar object (Wolff, 1960). During his first postnatal week, a hungry infant will briefly suck on everything which touches his lips, but at four weeks he no longer does so; he rejects those objects that touch his lips which are not a nipple (Piaget, 1936). This form of recognition, which Piaget terms "recognitory assimilation," continues to evolve, and in Piaget's second stage of sensori-motor development it encompasses intersensory coordinations and the "first acquired adaptations." During the second postnatal month the infant comes to suck what he sees, and position influences his nutritive sucking. In addition, the motor aspects of his behavior are enlarged to include new elements, such as new aspects of his search for the nipple. A passage from Piaget's original observations is illustrative:

> ... it seemed to us that accommodation to the breast itself made some progress during the second month and went beyond the reflex accommodation of the first weeks. We know that in Jacqueline from 0;1 (14) and in Lucienne from 0;1 (27) the natural disposition was to turn the head to the correct side when the breast was changed; whereas their body's rotation should have directed the head to the outside, they themselves turned it in the direction of the breast. Such behavior ... indicates that henceforth the child knows how to utilize the contacts with his mother's arms as signals enabling him to mark the location of the food. Now if this is the case, there is obviously acquired association, that is to say, accommodation which transcends simple reflex accommodation [1936, p. 58].

In other words, during the first sensorimotor stage the infant practices inborn behavior patterns which become more efficient and stabilized. Soon after, with the advent of the second sensorimotor stage, the infant begins to acquire new activities beyond the inborn patterns and, because of intersensory coordinations, he can "recognize" an object when he first makes contact with it. He no longer has to apply a reflex action pattern to it as in the first stage. To continue with examples from Piaget (1936), sucking itself as the only basis for recognition is progressively replaced by (1) a brief contact with the breast (leading to nutritional sucking), then later by (2) the sight of the breast, and later still by (3) the mother opening her dress. Early in the second stage various actions by the mother assume increasing importance in eliciting anticipatory feeding responses from the infant.

In the light of Piaget's sensorimotor theory, it is interesting that many mothers of our study felt their infants "knew" them when they were interviewed during the first and second months' visit. Their observations that such recognition occurred by virtue of feeding and soothing responsiveness may have been accurate reflections of their infants' adaptations in Piaget's sense. Certainly their responses are consistent with Piaget's observations and his conceptualizations about early recognitory assimilation. Yet this recognition is primitive, for it is still activated only by direct motor action elicited by the object. It is in no way independent of such action.

B. LATER RECOGNITION

In the third stage of sensorimotor development (about five to eight months), recognition still depends upon action in progress. Before eight months, there is typically no memory of an object once it disappears. If a favorite toy is moved away from the infant, he follows it with his eyes until it is made to disappear under a cloth. At that point, he shows no evidence of search behavior. Instead, he looks away from the cloth and we may see a blank, empty, or perplexed expression on his face. When this sequence is demonstrated repeatedly, even the most skeptical observer becomes convinced that, for the baby, "out of sight is out of mind."

It is only during the next stage, the fourth, that he can pursue the toy as it disappears, lift up the cloth, and find the toy. At this point (generally from eight to 13 months) out of sight is not out of mind; an object can be recognized, even though screened from the infant's perception. A mental image of a vanished object can be maintained for at least a brief time while he conducts a search. Yet there are still gross limitations on his ability to sustain any impression of the vanished object. The existence of that object is still closely tied to the action context in which it disappeared. If the toy is placed under one cloth, then moved while still in his sight to a place under another cloth, the infant will look for the toy in the place where he saw it disappear. The absent object is tied to a special position.

The ability to find the toy after "one visible displacement" is a property of the fifth stage. When this stage is reached, the object is no longer tied to the context of a previous action or special position but is now a product of his visual perception. However, even at this stage of development (generally from 13 to 18 months), the infant still cannot maintain the image of the object if it has a single "invisible displacement." If the toy is hidden under one cloth without the infant seeing it and then moved to a hidden position under a second cloth, he loses it. He will give up his search. He can sustain the mental image when the toy is moved from place to place so long as he sees it, but he cannot deduce its existence if he cannot see it being moved from one place to another.

Finally, as the culmination of sensorimotor development, in the sixth stage (around 16 to 18 months) the infant shows us that he can successfully search for an object which is hidden under one cloth and moved under a second cloth without his seeing it. Now he can deduce where the object is; it exists independently of his perception of it. He can *evoke* a representation of the absent object and pursue it. Now mental representation is freed from both the perception of the object and the action of pursuing it. Piaget subtitles this watershed stage in development "The invention of new means through mental combinations." As he says, "Henceforth there exists invention and no longer only discovery; there is, moreover, representation and no longer only sensorimotor groping" (1936, p. 341).

C. NEWER RESEARCH

It is striking that now, nearly four decades after Piaget's original formulations about infancy, we are in the midst of such a burgeoning research effort concerning them. Undoubtedly the current fashionability of Piaget's sensorimotor theory in the United States is partly a reflection of social action and the interest in compensatory education before the preschool year (see S. White, 1970). But, more than this, it is a tribute to the research richness of this theory. Since we began our research project, a number of other investigators have reported important findings about the infant's development of object permanence. One group has collected normative data and another has examined object permanence and compared its development with "person permanence."

Piaget's primary interest was in the creation of a system of "genetic epistemology." His sensorimotor theory was based on observations of his own three children, and these observations yielded descriptions of developmental stages, not normative data about the ages at which these stages begin. A number of recent investigators have now contributed these kinds of data (Décarie, 1962, 1974; Corman and Escalona, 1969; Miller, Cohen, and Hill, 1970; Bell, 1970; Gratch and Landers, 1971; Landers, 1971; Paraskevopoulos and Hunt, 1971; Wachs, Uzgiris, and Hunt, 1971; Ramsay, personal communication). However, in reviewing their results, a new complexity emerges. The "normative" age levels found by different investigators differ widely—so much that it seems unlikely that they can be accounted for by differences in the populations studied. Undoubtedly the conditions of testing, usually not reported in detail, play a more important role in the outcome of such measures than has heretofore been acknowledged. This in itself is an important area for future research. Meanwhile, our interpretation of current research is made more difficult, particularly in comparisons of one study with another.

The idea that cognitive development in connection with people might occur somewhat earlier than cognitive development in connection with inanimate objects, that "person permanence" might precede "object permanence," was originally suggested by Piaget (1936). It is now under active investigation. In her psychoanalytic discussion, Fraiberg (1969), while agreeing with the importance of this idea, expressed doubt that person permanence could precede object permanence by as much as eight to 10 months; in other words, it seems unlikely that evocative memory for the mother could be that far in advance of evocative memory for inanimate objects and thereby account for the onset of stranger distress. As of this writing, three investigations have been conducted on person permanence and object permanence (Décarie, 1962; Bell, 1970; Paradise and Curcio, 1974). The results indicate that person permanence does precede object permanence. One cross-sectional study (Paradise and Curcio, 1974) even found that 13 of the 15 infants who responded negatively to strangers between nine and 10 months had achieved stage six on the scale of person permanence! However, as exciting as these results are, the conditions of testing present even more complexities for the interpretation of results concerning person permanence than they do concerning object permanence. When the mother disappears behind the couch or behind other large objects designed to hide her, there are additional variables which are not present when a toy rattle disappears under a cloth. The mother's much larger size, her greater distance from the infant, her self-generated movement and noise, and different infant response criteria are only a few of the differences which make a comparison with the inanimate object series, originally used by Piaget, a difficult one.

Fraiberg (1969) has suggested that explanations of stranger distress onset may not require the presence of evocative memory but only the achievement of Piaget's fourth stage of sensorimotor development. Within the action context of the approaching person, the infant expects to recognize his mother's face, as he expects to find the toy under the cloth. Instead, his expectation is not met and distress ensues. If we accept this explanation, it would be sensorimotor stage four, where out of sight is not totally out of mind, that would be necessary before full-blown stranger distress could appear.

Our longitudinal study gave us an opportunity to test the proposed relationship between stage four of cognitive development and the onset of stranger distress. Specifically, we examined the hypothesis that the achievement of stage four of object permanence would be necessary before the full-blown response of stranger distress could occur. Beginning at four months, each home visit included a filmed testing for object permanence in the manner of Piaget. We used a favorite toy of the infant and cloth screens for covering it, and tested until the upper limits of the infant's abilities were clearly reached. After our study was completed, a rater, uninformed about our correlational interests, scored all films for test passes and failures. Onset of stranger distress was determined from two other independent raters' assessments of the filmed social-interaction series. Global judgments were used for this analysis, based upon observations of pronounced frowning, fussing, or crying in response to the stranger's approach.

The results were clear-cut. Of the 13 cases in which there were no data gaps in the monthly ratings, eight infants showed stranger distress before passing stage four; overt stranger distress occurred in the same session in which the infant failed to search for the hidden toy under the cloth. During these same sessions, infants were fully cooperative and able to follow the toy in the act of disappearing by looking after it (pass on stage 3 b, Piaget object permanence scale). Four infants passed stage four on a visit preceding the onset of stranger distress, and one infant initially passed stage four on the same visit as when stranger distress began.

Thus there does *not* appear to be a necessary sequence of passing stage four before manifesting stranger distress. In most instances, stranger distress occurred earlier, and, in fact, six of the eight infants in whom this happened did not pass stage four on the next monthly session, even though stranger distress occurred on that visit as well. The distribution of onset of stranger distress among our infants and our explanatory hypotheses for this phenomenon will be presented in the next two chapters.

CONCLUSION: A DEVELOPMENTAL SEQUENCE IN
THE AFFECTIVE RECOGNITION OF THE MOTHER

As early as two months of age, most mothers in our year-long study believed that their infants recognized them, primarily on the basis of individualized soothing and feeding responses. By four months, evidence that the infant "knew" his mother was apparent by virtue of greater smiling and motor responsiveness in her presence. During the early months, there was no evidence of distress in response to the approach of a stranger, but by eight to 10 months the approaching stranger could provoke crying. Antecedents of crying in this situation appeared during the three months preceding the overt response. We found evidence for a developmental sequence which began with a curious "comparing" of the mother's and the stranger's faces at five months and progressed to a sober staring at the stranger's face between five and seven months.

Piaget's sensorimotor theory is useful in conceptualizing the infant's developing discrimination of the mother from unfamiliar people. It offers explanations for our data in terms of early forms of "recogritory assimilation" and stages of object permanence. Our data do not support the hypothesis that stranger distress occurs only after the achievement of stage four of object permanence.

10

STRANGER DISTRESS
AND SEPARATION DISTRESS

The second half of the first year is a time of discoveries. The infant is highly curious, and his explorations show an increasing range. He not only searches with his eyes but grasps what he wants.

It is all the more striking, then, that in the midst of this positive approach tendency, negative reactions begin to occur. The infant is not without reserve in his explorations. Evidence of reserve is often prominent in social encounters with unfamiliar people. In such situations, he may no longer allow himself to be approached or picked up by friends of the family, new baby-sitters, or other unfamiliar people. He may frown, avert his gaze, and cry. He may even attempt a physical escape. This is especially dramatic when a grandmother, after a period of being away, holds out her hands to pick up her grandchild and to her dismay is greeted by a loud cry and frantic attempts to return to the mother.

Distress reactions to strangers were described by the early pioneers of infant observation (Preyer, 1888; Baldwin, 1895; Dearborn, 1910). They have been much discussed since, though it is only within the past 15 years that they have received concentrated systematic study. Many questions about these reactions have yet to be answered; in fact, even the basic question whether stranger distress is an expectable developmental event has not been settled. Most infant researchers seem to consider it as a developmental milestone, with a usual onset between seven and nine months of age (see discussions in Munsinger, 1971; Mussen, Conger, and Kagan, 1974). However, recently, its universality has been questioned on the basis of experimental data; a large number of infants at these ages were found to respond positively rather than negatively to strangers (Rheingold and Eckerman, 1973; Yarrow, 1967; Décarie, 1974).

Other questions are also prominent. Are such reactions primarily dependent on maturational factors? Or are they the result of learning, the infant having associated unfamiliar people with unpleasant events such as the mother's departure? What is the mode of onset of stranger distress? Is its appearance gradual or sudden? When it first appears does it persist over time, or is it sporadic and highly dependent upon situational context? A rapid onset with persistence might be more consistent with the hypothesis of "maturational readiness," whereas a gradual onset might suggest a learning explanation with social discrimination resulting from accumulating experience. To be sure, such evidence would not be conclusive, since maturation could progress slowly, or conversely, learning could occur in an abrupt fashion.

Another question emerges from current views about stranger distress. What is the correlation between stranger distress and separation distress? Ethological and psychoanalytic hypotheses about stranger distress have emphasized its relations to the formation of maternal attachment and to some kind of awareness or anticipation of maternal loss. Attachment theorists influenced by ethology have looked at stranger distress as one among a number of species-specific behavioral response systems which promote the establishment of social bonds between the infant and his primary caretaker (Bowlby, 1969, 1973; Schaffer, 1966; Hess, 1959; Moltz, 1960). When in distress, the infant tends to avoid the unfamiliar person or situation, and at the same time is motivated to seek comfort from his familiar caretaker.

Scott (1963) and Sluckin (1965), in discussing the animal literature, emphasized the temporal relationship between the onset of the fear of strangers and the termination of the period in which primary attachments can occur. The relationship between stranger distress and the establishment of specific maternal-infant bonds was also discussed by Spitz, who considered stranger distress to be, in the final analysis, a reaction to mother loss. He postulated that when the infant compared the unfamiliar face of the stranger to memory traces of the mother, anxiety resulted from the realization that this person was not the mother and that "mother is gone" (Spitz, 1959). High correlations of onset and intensity of separation and stranger distress would support the view that these two developmental phenomena are closely linked. Low correlations, on the other hand, would suggest independence, and would raise doubts about a common explanation for both.

These questions were studied by means of the already described social-interaction series (see Chapter 3 for details of method and scoring).

Stranger Distress: Expectable or Unpredictable?

The results of our study are fully consistent with the characterization of stranger distress as an expectable developmental event. All 14 infants manifested stranger distress in our social-interaction series during the first year. The mean age of onset was 8.4 months for the first stranger (mother absent) and 8.1 months for the second stranger (mother present) (range of onset was 5-12 months; 11 of the 14 infants manifested such distress by nine months). Data from maternal interviews provided a similar picture: the mean age of onset for stranger distress was 7.6 months (range, 5-10 months), though three infants showed only "equivocal" distress responses during the first year. Thus while eight months was the average age of onset, there was considerable variation among the infants. Though several investigators have described an earlier onset of stranger distress in females (Robson, Pedersen, and Moss, 1969; Schaffer, 1966), we found no indication of a sex difference in age of onset.

Why is it that some researchers do not regard stranger distress as an expectable developmental event? It has occurred to us that some of the contradictory data and conclusions may result from the application of cross-sectional data to a question which can be answered definitively only with a longitudinal design (Décarie, 1974). Because of the confusion in the literature, we feel it is worthwhile elaborating on this point. Studies showing that a large number of infants at a given age do not show distress have generally been cross-sectional (Rheingold and Eckerman, 1973; Scarr and Salapatek, 1970; Morgan and Ricciuti, 1969). Table M (see Appendix) displays our data cross-sectionally, showing the number of cases of stranger distress as measured by our global-impression rating for months five through 12. The proportion of infants showing stranger distress in any given month is similar to the proportion reported by others from cross-sectional studies. An increasing number of infants showed distress with increasing age, yet at any given month, approximately one half of the infants tested did not show distress. The contrast with a longitudinal view is striking. When our data were viewed longitudinally, all infants showed distress at one point or another. Other longitudinal studies also support the contention that stranger distress is an expectable developmental phenomenon. Schaffer (1966) found stranger distress in 34 of 36 infants followed monthly during the first year of life, with a range in onset of 25-48 weeks. The remaining two infants manifested stranger distress within the next six months. Tennes and Lampl (1964), also using a longitudinal design, observed stranger distress in 18 of the 19 infants in their study.

The results of our study also indicated that stranger distress was not a sporadic or evanescent phenomenon. Once it occurred, it tended to be elicited in the next month's visit:

after its onset, 11 of the 14 infants showed stranger distress two months consecutively, and eight showed stranger distress three months consecutively.

STRANGER DISTRESS: AGE TRENDS AND MODE OF ONSET

Figure 9 displays the mean stranger distress intensity scores for our 14 infants, derived from both film and interview data and measured by facial expression and gaze direction (see Table E in the Appendix). Though we felt justified in assuming that gaze behavior reflected the infant's affective state, objections could be raised to its inclusion in an intensity scale. Figure 10 therefore displays the course of stranger distress for ratings of facial expression alone. Both graphs show that maximal distress (represented in negative numbers) is reached at nine months and levels off during the rest of the first year. Up to five months, responses were highly positive, with smiling prominent. All infants smiled in response to the stranger at four months, and all but three infants at five months. By six months, positive responding had considerably diminished; a sober expression was characteristic up to eight months. By the ninth month, a definitely negative response was typical and persisted for the rest of the year.

Our finding of maximum distress at nine months replicates findings of other longitudinal studies which indicated that negative reactions peak before 10 months (Bayley, 1932; Spitz, 1950; Tennes and Lampl, 1964; Schaffer, 1966). But it is at variance with two cross-sectional studies in which stranger distress was found to increase in intensity over the first year (Morgan and Ricciuti, 1969; Scarr and Salapatek, 1970). How can we account for this difference? Again, it may result from inherent differences in longitudinal and cross-sectional approaches. Though most investigators have assumed that an experimental procedure repeated after intervals of at least a month would not be remembered and thus would not affect the infant's response, Morgan's suggestion that infants in

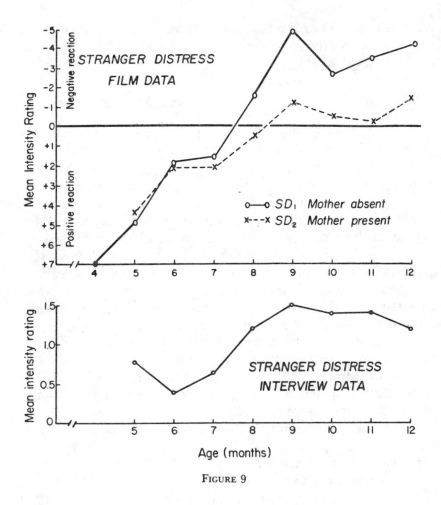

FIGURE 9

longitudinal studies become familiar with the experimental setting and thus give attenuated responses offers a possible explanation. Aside from memory of specific strangers, it might also be that older infants tested on only one occasion would be more sensitive to the highly unusual circumstances of an unfamiliar testing situation. Thus the laboratory environment, with its equipment, personnel, and implicit threats of separation, might enhance a potential for a distress response over and above any response to the stranger.

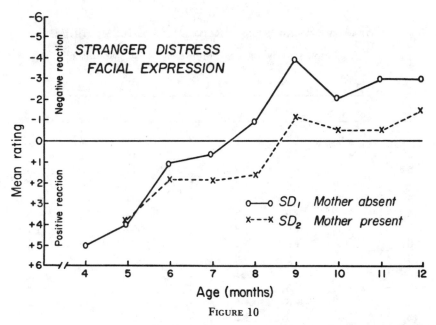

FIGURE 10

Data from our individual cases indicate that the onset of stranger distress is rapid. By far the largest increase in distress ratings occurred in the month leading up to the time of onset, with little increase thereafter. Table 6 shows the intensity scores (using facial expression and gaze direction) for the 14 infants in response to the first stranger in our social-interaction series. Data are arrayed according to month of onset of stranger distress. Nine of the 14 infants showed a large jump from essentially positive or sober responding to an unquestionably intense negative response.

There was still another indication of rapid onset: in nine of the 14 infants, stranger distress for the first stranger peaked within one month of onset. For the second stranger, our findings were less impressive, but in seven of the 14 infants stranger distress peaked within one month of onset.

In addition to facial expression, we rated gaze direction and motor activity. The course of gaze direction corresponded to the developmental shift in facial response. During the early months, uninterrupted attentiveness predominated. With age,

TABLE 6
STRANGER RESPONSE INTENSITY RATINGS EQUATED FOR MONTH OF ONSET

Case	Months preceding onset			Month of onset	Months following onset		
	-3	-2	-1	0	+1	+2	+3
1	+5	+1	+2	-2	-11	-7	-12
2	+5	0	0	-3	+4	+1	
3		+7	+7	-4	-4	-5	-5
4			+4	-1	0	-3	-7
5	+5	+6	+6	-8	-12	-10	-12
6		+8	+4	-10	-2	-3	+3
7	+9	+6	+3	-9	-5	-6	+1
8		+8	+7	-7	-9	-3	-1
9	-1	+3	0	-4			
10	0	0	-1	-4			
11	+7	+6	+6	-8	-10	-11	+8
12		+6	+6	-9	+2	-2	-5
13	+6	+9	+2	-8	-6		
14	+6	+7	+6	-4	-7	-9	

there evolved a pattern of looking toward the stranger and then away, usually proceeding back and forth. From the seventh month on, approximately one half of the infants showed absolute avoidance during at least one phase of the three-phase stranger approach. Table 7 is a contingency table which displays the concomitance of presence or absence of stranger distress with the presence of "toward" or "away" responses. An "away" response is four times more likely to be seen when distress is present; conversely, a "toward" response is far more likely in the absence of distress. It would seem that visual avoidance may be a part of the stranger response, and may reflect a means of coping with the unwelcome stimulus.

Our over-all motor activity ratings were unrevealing. As indicated in Chapter 3, this may have been due to problems inherent in our scale, as reflected in the low interrater reliability for this category. It may also be that over-all motor

TABLE 7
CONTINGENCY FOR "TOWARD" AND "AWAY" RESPONSES
OCCURRING IN PRESENCE OR ABSENCE OF STRANGER DISTRESS

| | Stranger Distress | |
	Present	Absent
"Toward" Responses	9	39
"Away" Responses	36	12

activity did not appreciably change either with age or with the phases of our experimental sequence.

SEPARATION DISTRESS: AGE TRENDS AND MODE OF ONSET

Both film and interview data indicated a different developmental course for separation distress during the first year than for stranger distress. Figure 11 shows a steadily increasing curve, apparently still rising in intensity at 12 months. Four infants manifested no separation distress during the first year. Four others showed separation distress only on the twelfth-month laboratory visit. Whereas the frequency of stranger distress, once present, was fairly consistent during the seven-to-12-month period, separation distress tended to occur much more erratically, to be isolated in time, and depended much more on the context of the separation (relative strangeness of the environment and the presence of exacerbating circumstances such as fatigue, illness, and previous experiences with separation). Of the two infants who showed early separation distress in the experimental sequences, one infant was in an obviously irritable state from an acute infection and a new tooth during a laboratory visit; the other was also teething and in the midst of a week's long cold during a home visit. The earliest example of separation distress noted in our interview material occurred at the age of four months and was asso-

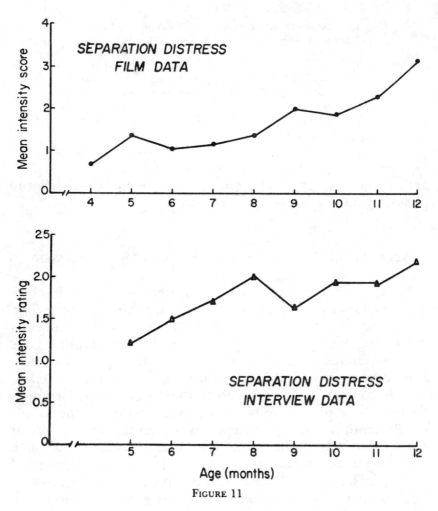

FIGURE 11

ciated with a room change and the mother's return to work. In general, by our measures, separation distress seemed to have the characteristics of a behavior in the process of differentiating, but not yet well established. Our findings are in agreement with Tennes and Lampl (1964), who found a similar course during the first year, with a peak intensity during the second year (13-18 months).

Separation Distress: Its
Relationship to Stranger Distress

Differing developmental curves suggested to us that stranger distress and separation distress are clearly separable phenomena with different developmental courses. Rank order correlations between stranger-distress variables and separation distress also supported this conclusion. Whereas statistically significant correlations were found between stranger distress for the first stranger and stranger distress for the second stranger, both for onset and intensity, there were no significant correlations involving separation distress. Specifically, there were no significant correlations between separation distress and stranger distress for either stranger, in either onset or intensity. In the light of these data, it seems difficult to maintain the notion of a simple relationship between stranger distress and either fear of maternal loss or "attachment behavior," to the extent that either of these is measured by separation distress.

The earlier notion that stranger distress is primarily an expression of fear of maternal loss seems no longer tenable. It is hard to reason that the infant shows distress in response to a situation in which he must infer a loss (i.e., stranger = prospective mother-loss) when he fails to show any distress in response to the actual loss itself (mother leaving). In our study, 62% of all cases of stranger distress occurred without prior separation distress. Furthermore, stranger distress occurred in the mother's presence with high frequency at expectable ages. Stranger distress in the mother's presence was observed 39 times in our social-interaction series. It occurred at least once in all infants, and accounted for 45% of all observed instances of stranger distress. Indeed, most of the recent studies of stranger distress have used a stranger approach with the mother present, and have found incidences of stranger distress quite similar to ours (Schaffer, 1966; Tennes and Lampl, 1964; Morgan and Ricciuti, 1969; Scarr and Salapatek, 1970).

While not explaining stranger distress per se, it seems clear from our data that separation from the mother does sensitize the infant to the stranger, either intensifying the distress response or lowering its threshold. For example, when separation distress was present in the sequence, stranger distress almost always followed. Of 20 instances of separation distress, 17 were followed by distress in response to the second stranger (mother present). The fact that, from the sixth month on, for every month the response to the stranger was rated as more negative in the mother's absence also strongly suggests that the mother's absence does have a sensitizing effect (Figure 9).

Product-moment correlations between intensity scores for the various experimental sequences (separation, stranger in mother's absence, stranger in mother's presence) also support the notion that stranger distress is a phenomenon independent from separation distress, though enhanced by the mother's absence. There were three categories of correlations: stranger distress 1 (mother absent) with stranger distress 2 (mother present) (SD-1/SD-2); separation distress with stranger distress 1 (Sep/SD-1); separation distress with stranger distress 2 (Sep/SD-2) (see Table 8). As would be expected if the stranger is the overriding variable, the highest mean correlation was between distress in response to the first stranger and distress in response to the second stranger. This hypothesis is also supported by the finding that correlations between the two stranger sequences reached the .05 level of significance in seven of eight months measured. At the same time, there were consistently higher correlations between separation and stranger distress in the mother's absence than between separation and stranger distress in the mother's presence (higher mean correlations, as well as more correlations at the .05 level). The higher correlations between stranger distress in the mother's absence and separation distress suggest that the common factor of separation does influence the stranger response and probably contributes to the increased intensity seen in the mother's absence for most of the months studied.

TABLE 8

CORRELATIONS BETWEEN INTERACTION SEQUENCES
Stranger 1 with Stranger 2 (SD-1/SD-2)
Separation with Stranger 1 (Sep/SD-1)
Separation with Stranger 2 (Sep/SD-2)

1. *Rho's across cases by month* [*5 through 12*]

Months	SD-1/SD-2	Sep/SD-1	Sep/SD-2
5	+ .641*	+ .068	+ .015
6	+ .661**	+ .483	+ .672**
7	+ .702**	+ .623*	+ .477
8	+ .689**	-.190	-.201
9	+ .736**	+ .561*	+ .320
10	+ .395	+ .574*	+ .462*
11	+ .562*	+ .320	+ .208
12	+ .527*	+ .590*	+ .377
Mean	+ .614	+ .379	+ .291

* Significant at .05 level
** Significant at .01 level

Since our social-interaction series involved an invariant sequence, an argument could be made that high correlations between the stranger sequences reflect not simply stranger distress but a sensitization of the infant to a succession of "stressful" experiences. In other words, order effects might account for the results rather than differing qualities inherent in the separation and stranger experiences. A subsequent study focusing on the behavioral and heart-rate responses of five- and nine-month-old infants to a stranger approach sequence (to be detailed in Chapter 11) included a design which enabled us to test for order effects, as well as the effects of the mother's presence or absence, on the intensity of stranger distress. Results indicated that a "sensitization" or "mood effect" was influential in the experimental sequences. In each sequence, the infant showed increased distress on the approach of a second stranger, independent of the mother's presence or absence and of the placement of the separation sequence. As was suggested by our longitudinal study, the mother's absence also served as a sensitizing factor. In addition, one of the results of this cross-sectional study supported inferences drawn in our previous discussion: the frequencies of stranger distress, when present, were similar to those reported in other cross-sectional studies.

CORRELATIONS BETWEEN FUSSINESS, STRANGER DISTRESS, AND SEPARATION DISTRESS

In Chapter 7 we offered a speculative hypothesis about early unexplained fussiness, proposing that it evolved in our species for purposes of enhancing attachment. We thought it worthwhile to examine the degree of correlation between the intensity of early fussiness and the intensity of stranger distress and/or separation distress, both of which have been considered in the literature as indicators of attachment. If such a hypothesis were correct, one might expect high positive correlations between the intensity of fussiness and the intensity of later distress. One might also expect positive correlations between the intensity of fussiness and early onset of later distress variables.

The data did not support the hypothesis regarding fussiness and attachment as measured by separation distress. Rank order correlations between fussiness and all parameters of separation distress (onset and intensity) during the first year were extremely low, both for the film and interview data. Certainly there appeared to be no obvious or necessary relationship between early fussiness and the later intolerance of separation during the first year.

Since we found that stranger distress was not highly correlated with separation distress, it would seem inappropriate to look for correlations between stranger distress and fussiness in support of an "attachment" hypothesis. However, some significant positive correlations did emerge between fussiness and stranger distress variables. This suggested that there was individual consistency in distress reactiveness.

CONCLUSION: A DEVELOPMENTAL
EVENT REQUIRING EXPLANATION

Our data strongly support the idea that stranger distress is an expectable developmental event. Its onset is generally around seven to nine months, though with considerable individual variation, and its appearance is relatively abrupt, full intensity being reached soon after onset. Stranger distress was observed to have a separate developmental course from separation distress. The low statistical correlations between parameters of separation and stranger distress suggest that fear of mother loss is not a sufficient explanation for the appearance of stranger distress, nor is there any simple chronological relationship between attachment measured by separation distress and stranger distress.

But how can we explain stranger distress? We must admit that this question remains unanswered. As we have already pointed out (see Chapter 9), a cognitive explanation is also insufficient. In addition to the unconvincing sequential relationship between stranger distress and the passage of stage four on the Piaget object permanence scale, there are other problems. A cognitive explanation fails to explain why the infant has not shown stranger distress earlier than seven or eight months despite the ability to discriminate adequately between the mother and unfamiliar people, an ability which can be observed three or four months earlier. It also fails to explain why some cognitively "discrepant" stimuli should provoke distress and avoidance while other stimuli elicit curious exploration or inattention and lack of interest. Our current working explanation for the development of this phenomenon implies some major reorientation in our thinking. It is the topic of the next chapter.

11

A HYPOTHESIS ABOUT
FEARFULNESS AND A
NEW LEVEL OF ORGANIZATION

Stranger distress, when it occurs, is a startling and puzzling phenomenon. An unfamiliar person, approaching the child in a friendly fashion, is suddenly greeted with a cry of distress. Why? In the previous chapter, we discussed several constraints on theorizing about the meaning of this heightened selectiveness. Stranger distress is not explained on the basis of maternal loss, nor is it fully accounted for by any current cognitive explanation.

A HYPOTHESIS

We believe that the infant's developing attachment to his mother and his developing cognitive capacities are of obvious importance in the emergence of stranger distress. But more is needed to explain its occurrence. We hypothesize that the added factor is a maturational one and that it controls a further differentiation of emotionality, namely the onset of a capacity for "fearfulness." This hypothesis, though in a somewhat different form, has also been suggested by Schaffer (1966) and by Scarr and Salapatek (1970). A second aspect of our hypothesis follows from the genetic field theory as well as from our research data. It is that fearfulness itself reflects a more general organismic shift—a shift to a new level of organization, one that is apparent not only in the emotional sector but in physiological and social sectors.

In the first part of this chapter we will discuss evidence for the aspect of our hypothesis that deals with the onset of fearfulness. In the second part we will discuss evidence for the organismic shift, as well as its importance for the infant and his family.

The Onset of Fearfulness

It seems to us that the scientific literature on fearfulness can be marshaled in support of the hypothesis that a fear system develops in the human at approximately seven to nine months. Evidence is of two sorts. First, there is evidence concerning the maturational control of the responses which are presumed to be part of such a system, and second, there is evidence concerning the onset of fearfulness in response to stimuli other than strange people. We will also briefly review what is known about the onset of fearfulness in animals. If our hypothesis about maturation is correct, we might expect a phylogenetic history.

A. EVIDENCE FROM STUDIES OF STRANGER DISTRESS

A number of studies have pointed to the seven-to-nine-month period as the expectable time for the onset of stranger distress (Buhler, 1930; Spitz, 1950; Freedman, 1961; Tennes and Lampl, 1964; Schaffer, 1966; Morgan and Ricciuti, 1969; Scarr and Salapatek, 1970; Ainsworth, 1967; Stevens, 1971). That such consistent results have been found in so many different countries in infants who have experienced a variety of different rearing conditions is strong evidence that maturational factors are crucial in determining time of onset. Ainsworth (1967), for example, in a longitudinal study of Ugandan infants, found that they typically began to show distress in her presence in the third quarter of the first year. The findings of Stevens (1971), who studied infants raised in a foundling home in Greece, were similar: at least half of the infants developed stranger distress, the mean age of onset being 8.4 months.

Further evidence for the maturational or genetic control of this response comes from Freedman's twin study. In a well-controlled longitudinal study involving 20 sets of twins seen monthly during the first year of life, he compared the onset and course of stranger distress in monozygotic and dizygotic pairs of twins. Zygocity was determined by blood typing only after the study was completed, and stranger distress was scored independently by judges who rated twins separately on the basis of films. Freedman found a significantly higher concordance for the onset of fear of strangers in identical twins than in fraternal twins. In addition, the developmental curves for stranger distress throughout the first year were often strikingly similar in the monozygotic pairs but not in the dizygotic pairs (Freedman, 1965, 1971).

Further support for a maturational hypothesis comes from negative findings: there is as yet no convincing evidence that learning affects the onset or intensity of this phenomenon. In the various studies reported there has been little correlation between stranger distress and experiential variables. Morgan and Ricciuti (1969) found little correlation between environmental variables and the manifestation of stranger distress in their experimental sequence. Schaffer (1966) found low correlations between stranger distress and all maternal relationship variables. The abrupt onset of stranger distress without observable environmental influence is also compatible with a maturationally determined event. Of course, support of our hypothesis would be immeasurably strengthened by evidence correlating specific maturational developments in the central nervous system with the behavioral changes. At present, such evidence is not available.

B. EVIDENCE FROM STUDIES OF FEARFULNESS IN RESPONSE TO OTHER STIMULI

Recent studies support the idea that fearfulness in response to strangers is one example of a more general capacity for fearfulness in response to many stimuli. Using a cross-sectional design, Scarr and Salapatek (1970) studied the patterns of fear development in infants between the ages of two and 23 months. They used six stimuli: strangers, the visual cliff, a jack-in-the-box, a mechanical dog, a mask, and loud noises. They saw little fearful responding to any of these stimuli before seven months; after seven months, the infants were found to respond with fear, the responses to the different stimuli having somewhat different developmental curves. Though from their cross-sectional data only tentative inferences about the onset of fear responses can be made, the authors have speculated that there is a developmental shift in the capacity to manifest fear at this time. The seven-to-nine-month period is also one in which behavioral fearfulness has been noted in response to the visual cliff apparatus (Schwartz, Campos, and Baisel, 1973) and to the "loom zoom" apparatus (Hruska and Yonas, 1972). This age has also been one during which unfamiliar situations seem for the first time to produce distress. Bayley (1932) noted this with regard to the surroundings for developmental testing and Rheingold (1969) in regard to unfamiliar playroom surroundings. Paradise and Curcio (1974) found that nine-to-10-month-old infants who responded negatively to strangers were more likely to respond negatively to other new situations; this was thought to represent "a general tendency to approach new social and non-social situations with displeasure" in infants of this age.

In a recent longitudinal study of the onset of "wariness," Schaffer, Greenwood, and Parry (1972) studied the reactions of infants to the introduction of an incongruous object after a familiarization procedure with another similar object. The objects used were two small plastic cones of different colors Up to eight months, Schaffer et al. observed an "immediate approach" tendency which was independent of the degree of familiarity of the object. After eight months, a relatively prolonged hesitation was noted before the infants contacted the unfamiliar stimulus. Though they considered the onset of "wariness" to reflect the influence of developing memory stores on the infant's expressive behavior, an explanation involving the maturation of a "fear system" with motivational properties may also be important. It is interesting, in the light of our finding of the abrupt onset of stranger distress, that the onset of "wariness" also occurred abruptly. Schaffer et al. state: ". . . the phenomenon was found in its fully developed form at nine months, having been completely absent at eight months" (1972, p. 173).

C. THE ONSET OF FEARFULNESS IN ANIMALS

Without making claims to a thorough review of the animal literature, we believe there is support for the notion that there is a development of a capacity for fearfulness, determined by maturational factors, and offering a possible phylogenetic history for the human. Most animals do not show fear at birth, yet at some later point in their development they evidence avoidance or "flight" behavior in response to certain stimuli. For example: birds show a fear and flight response at approximately 24 hours (Freedman, 1961; King, 1966; Hess, 1959); cats show fear of strangers in novel situations at five weeks (Collard, 1967); dogs show a fear of novel situations and human caretakers beginning around five to seven weeks (Freedman, King, and Elliot, 1961; Scott, 1963); monkeys manifest fear in response to novel stimuli at two to five months (Jacobsen, Jacobsen, and Yoshioka, 1932; Hebb and Reisen, 1943; Welker, 1956; Bernstein and Mason, 1962). That the development of fearful responding has an expectable time of onset in each of these species seems further evidence for a system in some ways dependent upon maturational factors for its flowering.

A longitudinal study of the development of fearfulness in

rhesus monkeys conducted by Sackett (1966) provides perhaps the most dramatic and convincing evidence for the independent development of fearfulness under maturational influence. Sackett raised eight rhesus monkeys in total social isolation from birth. Once a week each was shown the same set of slide-projected photographs of other monkeys in various poses. Beginning at two to two and a half months and peaking at two and a half to three months, pictures of monkeys in threat postures resulted in increased distress vocalizations and other disturbance behaviors. The disturbance behaviors, which consisted primarily of "fear, withdrawal, rocking, and huddling," were observed rarely, if at all, before two months, and appeared to wane by four to five months. Pictures of monkeys in other forms of activity did not provoke such responses.

A New Level of Organization

The concept of fearfulness onset implies a new level of organization. In the previous chapter, we used "distress" as a descriptive term for the infant's behavior: namely, his negative response to an approaching stranger. We wished to avoid assumptions about the infant's subjective state. But in this chapter we have introduced the concept of fearfulness. We believe there is sufficient evidence that there has been a qualitative shift to a higher level of complexity, and that "fearfulness" describes this new level of organization better than does "distress." Let us review some of the evidence.

Before this time, distress has been of a nonspecific nature. Most commonly, it has been associated with physical discomfort, such as pain, changes in body temperature, uncomfortable positions, or hunger. Now, there is distress in response to *specific* patterned environmental stimuli. Such stimuli are predominantly in the visual and auditory modalities, and they produce behavioral responses which the observer naturally associates with fear, that is, *distress* and *physical attempts at avoidance*. There is a new quality in the distress response which is also manifest in another characteristic. More often than not, the observer is impressed by its occurrence in two phases: an initial phase (cognitive) of evaluation and a subsequent phase (motor) of distress and attempts at avoidance. The initial part of the response is typically spent in several seconds of looking and scanning; it is only afterward that overt distress is expressed. Still another feature strikes us about the new quality in the distress response. Reactions to stimuli are in the moderate intensity range rather than at the extremes, suggesting that it is the *meaning* of the stimulus which is important rather than the level of or change in stimulation.

From the point of view of social communication, there is also evidence that "fearfulness" is differentiating at this time. The facial expressions of infants showing distress in response to a stranger were identified by mothers and observers alike as those associated with "fearfulness." Adjectives such as "afraid," "frightened," and "wary" were commonly used in spontaneous descriptions. The extent to which the facial expressions which were identified as fearful differ from the facial expressions of earlier distress elicited in other circumstances is a matter for future research. We would hypothesize that there are subtle but definite differences. (See Ekman, Friesen, and Ellsworth [1972] for a review of such research in adults.)

Thus developmental changes in both the stimulus and response characteristics suggest further differentiation of emotionality. Let us now examine some evidence concerning shifts in other sectors of development.

A. A PHYSIOLOGICAL SHIFT: THE HEART-RATE RESPONSE

Recent research concerning the development of heart-rate responsiveness supports the hypothesis that there is a biobehavioral shift during this age period. But more than this, it gives another dimension to the argument that there is a shift from nonspecific distress to fearfulness at this time, with a link-up of cognitive discrimination, an affective response, and cardiac responsiveness.

Schwartz, Campos, and Baisel (1973) compared five- and nine-month-old infants for their behavioral and cardiac responsiveness to the visual cliff apparatus. This apparatus consists of a transparent plane which, because of the checkerboard pattern underneath it, can give to someone on top of it the illusion of being supported (the shallow side of the cliff) or of being unsupported (the deep side of the cliff). When five-month-olds were placed on the deep side of the cliff, their looking was associated with cardiac deceleration and there was no behavioral distress. When nine-month-olds were placed on the deep side, their looking was accompanied by cardiac acceleration, and often with overt distress.

In an attempt to further our knowledge about this kind of shift, we recently joined forces with Campos and his group. Using the approaching stranger as a stressful stimulus instead of the visual cliff, we studied 80 infants under experimental conditions which involved continuous time-locked monitoring of both behavior (by 16 mm. filming) and heart rate (by polygraph). As in the earlier study of Schwartz et al., infants were either five or nine months old. Figure 12 illustrates one aspect of our results: there was a dramatic shift from cardiac deceleration at five months to cardiac acceleration at nine months in response to the approach of the stranger. The abscissa of the graph is labeled according to sequential gradations of "entry" (stranger 12 feet away from the infant), "approach" (stranger five feet away from the infant), "intrude" (stranger two feet away from the infant), and "depart." Each gradation was divided into five three-second segments for purposes of analysis. The results shown are for 40 infants studied under the condition of a first stranger's approach with the mother absent; other conditions of a first stranger's approach with the mother present and of a second stranger's approach have been presented elsewhere

(Campos et al., 1975). Germane to our present discussion is the fact that a behavioral shift accompanied the cardiac shift that occurred between five and nine months. A typical five-month-old response was an expression of delighted curiosity. A nine-month-old response, on the other hand, was often one of sobriety which evolved to frowning and then crying with gaze aversion. Furthermore, it was not uncommon for the cardiac acceleration to precede the onset of crying by several seconds, illustrating that the heart-rate shift often anticipated crying and was not merely a consequence of it.

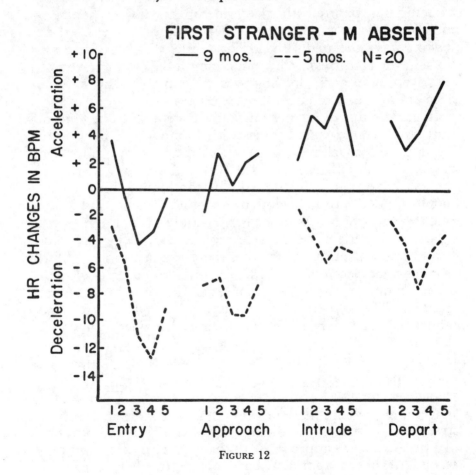

FIGURE 12

Further information about this kind of shift has been recorded by Hruska and Yonas (1972). They noted developmental changes in heart-rate responsiveness using an apparatus which creates the visual impression of impending collision, the so-called "loom zoom" apparatus. They found that cardiac deceleration associated with quieting and visual orientation was the rule in infants of two through seven months old. Initial deceleration followed by cardiac acceleration was typical of their group of infants at eight through 10 months old. Hruska and Yonas interpret this shift as reflecting the onset of a "defensive response."

B. A SOCIAL SHIFT: A NEW MESSAGE TO THE MOTHER

The social aspects of fearfulness give further emphasis to the idea of a shift to a new level of organization.

The message given by stranger distress is not just fearfulness. It is more; something like: "I feel secure only with you, mother. Please don't leave me alone with strange people." It is a different order of communication than the distress vocalizations and the smiling of earlier months; earlier affective expressions were not as compellingly directed toward a particular person. Furthermore, the new message has two components. On the one hand, there are certain situations which upset the infant. On the other hand, only the mother's presence will bring comfort. These are highly charged affective communications and, as such, evoke a variety of feelings in the mother. Some mothers in our longitudinal study responded with pleasure to this demonstration of special need. They took considerable pride in the fact that their infants preferred them and turned to them in moments of distress. Other mothers became uneasy about the degree of responsibility which seemed to accompany this special reliance. One mother expressed concern that her child was becoming a "momma's boy"; another wished that her little girl would soon become more "independent." But regardless of individual differences, the development of fearfulness in response to strangers, with its message of preference, introduced a new mode of relating for both mother and child. A special aspect of this mode has to do with the new meaning of separation.

C. A SHIFT IN THE MEANING OF SEPARATION: FEARFULNESS IN THE MIDST OF LOSS

Two clinical studies have highlighted a shift in the meaning of infant-mother separations during the period under discussion. Beginning with the third quarter of the first year, loss of the mother is considered to have severe consequences for the infant. Spitz and Wolf (1946) described the syndrome of anaclitic depression as one consequence of infant-mother separation during the second half of the first year. The syndrome, characterized by apprehension, weepiness, withdrawal from the environment, retardation of development, diminished activity, loss of appetite, and insomnia, was not observed in any infant younger than six months. This age, according to Spitz, is a critical one, after which separation from the mother cannot be tolerated by the infant since other caretakers cannot easily be substituted. Schaffer and Callender (1959) studied hospitalized infants and found similar age-related reactions. There was a marked shift in the infant's reaction to hospitalization before and after the age of seven months. Before that age, separation from the mother elicited little protest, strangers' attentions were accepted in the hospital, and the infant's return home was marked by only brief upsets. After seven months, responses were not nearly so tranquil. Typically, separation from the mother evoked vigorous protests, and members of the hospital staff would be greeted with signs of distress, negativism, and withdrawal. According to the authors, the return home marked a difficult readjustment period, during which there was a "great deal of insecurity centering around the presence of mother."

Both of these studies emphasize the loss of the mother and its timing as important in producing these syndromes. However, less emphasized has been the possibility that the maturational onset of the capacity for fearful responding may contribute to the clinical picture. When an infant is hospitalized, he is not only separated from the mother, he is forced to deal with a complement of strangers, a strange environment, and a variety of new and possibly painful procedures. The distressing consequences of losing the mother may not wholly be accounted for by the experience of separation itself. The mother is unavailable as a soother in the face of stimuli which for the first time may be experienced as "frightening." In Spitz's study of anaclitic depression, infants were made fearful to a pathological degree by situations which normal infants would find frightening but manageable. For example, whereas stranger distress in the normal child could be overcome in a short time, in these separated infants "desperate screaming" persisted, and they were inconsolable for as long as two or three hours. In the Schaffer and Callender hospitalization study, the abrupt onset of the hospitalization reactions, as commented on by the authors, may be explained not so much by the establishment of attachment to the mother as by a maturational "flowering" of fearful responding. This kind of explanation, which in some ways parallels our discussion of a maturational "flowering" of smiling, may even account in part for the abrupt onset of "attachment" in Schaffer and Emerson's (1964) longitudinal study. Their measures of attachment were derived from such situations as being left outside of the store, being left with strangers, and being left outside of the house. We suggest that these situations may have fear-producing aspects which are independent of the mother's presence or absence.

It is interesting that our thoughts about fearfulness in the midst of loss find some roots in Freud's (1926) description of infantile separation anxiety in "Inhibitions, Symptoms and Anxiety." In his formative work of ego psychology, Freud postulated that anxiety, even in infancy, is a signal of a dangerous separation. The infant, separated from his mother, becomes vulnerable to a flood of unmanageable stimuli;

anxiety signals a danger, it portends helplessness, because the mother is not available to gratify, protect, or soothe. Is it not possible that the disorganizing stimuli to which Freud referred could arise not only from the inside, from drive sources, but also from the outside, from fear-evoking stimuli?

CONCLUSION

That the onset of stranger distress is under maturational control seems consistent not only with our work but with that of others. The more speculative aspect of our hypothesis — that the onset of a general capacity for fearful responding is under similar control — also finds support. In addition, we conclude that the evidence supports the usefulness of the notion of a second biobehavioral shift to a new level of organization. Although the evidence for this is not as abundant as it is for the first biobehavioral shift, it seems promising. There are shifts in emotional organization as well as concomitant shifts in heart-rate responsiveness and the social meaning of fearfulness.

The infant's ability to communicate fear and his heightened preference for the mother undoubtedly serve adaptive purposes. They provide a safeguarding communication system in situations which are potentially threatening, and they begin to make possible the intense interpersonal bonding that is characteristic of the human species. At the same time, these advances carry with them certain vulnerabilities. Reliance on a single caretaker means the risk of a more devastating effect if that caretaker is lost or for some reason unable to meet the infant's increased expression of need. Likewise, the capacity to view certain stimuli as threatening carries with it the possibility that such stimuli can be overwhelming, both physiologically and psychologically.

12

OTHER ASPECTS OF
LATER AFFECT EXPRESSIONS

The affect expressions of the older baby are not "unexplained." By the second half of the first year, affect expressions have become a varied and effective means of communication. Although mothers often respond to affect signals automatically and without awareness, they are seldom puzzled by their message or meaning. In the expanding infant world, emotional expression remains a primary means whereby the preverbal infant conveys his wants.

Against this backdrop of increasingly effective communications, several aspects of later affectivity puzzled us. One aspect was the reappearance of prolonged nonhunger fussiness in several infants. This had some of the characteristics of early fussiness, but differed in a major respect which mothers helped us understand. Another aspect was the absence of fussiness where we expected it, namely, during weaning and teething. Instead, we were often met with indications of increasing exploratory behavior and involvement of the infant with his expanding world.

LATER FUSSINESS

A curve of mean ratings for fussiness during the first year was presented in Chapter 7. Highest ratings for fussiness were found in the early months, with a dip at three months and a gradual decline to almost zero at six months. The mean curve was found to be composed of three distinct temporal patterns of early fussiness (see Figures 6 and 7).

Five episodes of later fussiness occurred in five infants. Later fussiness was defined by a rating of two or more for longer than three days occurring any time after three months of age. The mean duration of these episodes was three weeks. Analysis of these later episodes proved most interesting. The ages at which they occurred sorted the infants into three clear groups, groups which exactly coincided with the three patterns of early fussiness described in Chapter 7. Infants of Pattern A, the *early pattern* (N = 2), had the earliest episodes of later fussiness, with age of onset ranging from three and a half to five months. Infants of Pattern B, the *intermediate pattern* (N = 2), also had an intermediate age of onset of later fussiness, namely at eight and nine months. The fifth infant was one who was of Pattern C, the *prolonged pattern;* he had the latest decline in fussiness and also the latest onset of a later fussiness episode: it began at 10 months. This temporal patterning suggested to us that there is a relationship between the age of decline of early prolonged, nonhunger fussiness and the age of onset of the isolated instances of later fussiness: there seems to be a continued sensitive period in which there may be a recrudescence of fussiness, and which extends almost three months after the decline of the earlier fussiness.

Our analysis of factors associated with these later episodes of fussiness was even more revealing. Unlike early prolonged, nonhunger fussiness, mothers had explanations for the later episodes of fussiness. From our independently coded categories of "potential stress events" we discovered that a "marked change in environment" was associated with the onset of each of these later conditions of fussiness. In one case, there was a two-week out-of-state visit to relatives. In another case, the infant's mother went to the hospital for five days, following which there was also a two-week visit to out-of-state relatives. In a third case, home remodeling resulted in the infant's being moved to a basement room with a totally different surround.

A fourth infant's late episode of fussiness was associated with a family move to another part of the city. In the fifth instance the mother began baby-sitting for five other children during the daytime, a situation which lasted for five weeks. In all cases the mothers spontaneously attributed the fussiness to a dramatic change in the environment, with a consequent disruption in the infant's routine and often with an expressed "disruption" in the mother's caretaking routine as well. Table 9 summarizes all scored instances of "marked change in environment" occurring after the decline of early fussiness. Although such environmental changes continued to occur throughout the infant's first year, they were associated with a recrudescence of prolonged fussiness only within three months after the decline of the early "unexplained fussiness."

TABLE 9
MARKED CHANGES IN ENVIRONMENT (MCE) IN RELATION TO LATER
PROLONGED FUSSINESS

Month after decline in "unexplained fussiness"	MCE associated with later fussiness onset	Total MCE	No. cases under one year during that month
1	1	2	14
2	3	6	14
3	1	2	13
4	0	1	12
5	0	6	12
6	0	5	12
7	0	1	9
8	0	3	6
9	0	1	5
10	0	2	1

That a change in the infant's physical environment, with its associated changes in caretaker routine, should be associated with distress should not surprise us in view of the findings of Burns et al. (1972). These investigators found that infants who experienced a change in a caretaker during the first two months responded with a significant increase in distress, as measured during sampled observation times during feedings. The salient feature in our data is that not all infants responded to all marked changes of environment at all times with prolonged fussiness. Only some infants responded (a question of individual differences) and only during a certain vulnerable time (within three months after the decline of early unexplained fussiness). An interaction of maturational and experiential factors seems likely and needs illumination from further research.

TEETHING AND WEANING

Whereas the fussiness associated with "marked change in environment" was unanticipated, there were other events which we expected would be associated with fussiness. Teething and feeding changes (i.e., introduction of solids, weaning from breast to bottle, and weaning from bottle to cup) have traditionally been considered stressful experiences for the child with a potential for emotional distress. Surprisingly, these events were not associated with prolonged fussiness.

In our 14 infants, a mean of five teeth per infant had erupted by the end of the first postnatal year. The earliest erupted at four months.

For one third of these teeth *no* days of fussiness were ratable on our scale within one week of the eruption. The remaining two thirds of the teeth were associated with fussiness, but in most instances it lasted only one day. The longest duration of fussiness was four days (one instance), but in only one seventh of all instances did fussiness last longer than one day.

Our data gave no indication that early teeth were more likely to be associated with fussiness than later teeth. When fussiness did occur with early teeth, however, it lasted longer: the mean duration of fussiness per tooth eruption during four through eight months was one day, whereas the mean duration of fussiness per tooth during nine through 12 months was one third of a day.

Three categories of feeding changes were examined in relation to fussiness. The age range during which solids were introduced in our cases was from two weeks to three months. Fussiness diminished within one week following such introduction in six cases, stayed the same within one week afterward in six cases, and increased within one week afterward in two cases. Thus there was no indication of an association between the introduction of solids and an increase in fussiness. This replicates a finding in the initial longitudinal study (Tennes et al., 1972).

Eleven of the 14 mothers in our study started breast feeding immediately after birth. One mother continued throughout the entire year, and another discontinued breast feeding during the first month. The mean age of weaning from the breast was approximately five months. In eight of the 10 infants who were weaned during the first year, there was no change in fussiness within one week afterward. In one case, fussiness diminished and in one case it increased within one week afterward. The cup was introduced as early as five months. One infant was not introduced to the cup during the first year. The mean age of introduction of the cup was eight months. In nine of the 13 infants no changes in fussiness occurred within one week afterward. In three infants the cup was associated with an increase in fussiness, and in one with a decrease. We therefore concluded that our data gave no indication that the introduction of solids, weaning from the breast, or introduction of the cup is associated with an increase in fussiness.

We also looked at those instances of anorexia or regurgitation reported by the mothers. Admittedly this is a more subjective category than the others since it relied upon the mothers' recalling significant "disturbances" rather than specific events. Although there were many instances of feeding disturbances reported throughout the course of the study, none were reported within one week after the breast was discontinued or after solids or cup feeding were introduced. Most of the feeding disturbances were found to be associated with mild or moderate systemic illnesses, primarily upper respiratory infections.

ACTIVITY AND CURIOSITY: A COUNTERTENDENCY TO FEARFULNESS

Not only was there little evidence of disturbance around the time of weaning, but several mothers commented on the pleasure with which their infants responded to the cup. Their infants seemed to enjoy manipulating and learning to use the cup, without showing any distress at relinquishing the former means of feeding. In fact, as we listened, observed, and tested, we could not help being impressed by the forward thrust in development that often appeared as a response to this change. We were reminded of what has been discussed theoretically as pleasure in functioning (*Funktionslust;* Bühler, 1918), as mastery (Hendrick, 1934), and as effectance motivation (R. White, 1963).

If we were to leave the reader with a picture of later infancy as a time of fearfulness and distress it would be a gross distortion. The ease with which our infants made the transition from the nipple to the cup was typical of an aspect of development which we found consistently impressive: namely, the infant's energetic attempts to explore and master his expanding world. Far more impressive than fearfulness was the curiosity and seeming enthusiasm with which infants ventured forth into new situations. Whereas earlier most seeking was by visual means, now crawling and in some cases walking added dramatic emphasis to this sector of development. The phrase "He's into everything" was repeated by one mother after another, and seemed to characterize a good deal of behavior. This aspect of development, along with the interrelationships between social and inanimate stimulation, is a subject of increasing research (Yarrow et al., 1975).

Over-all, the last few months of the first year seem to reflect a solidification of processes set in motion with the development of fearfulness and mother-infant attachment. The infant continues to explore and expand his world. He continues to have to deal with uncertain situations, but now, to an increasing degree, he uses the mother as a "secure base" (Ainsworth, Salter, and Wittig, 1969) from whom increasing distance can be tolerated. Toward the very end of our study period, we saw harbingers of the second year: the beginnings of confrontations with discipline, increasing protest at separation, and the beginnings of a few words.

13

OVERVIEW: THE ORGANIZATION OF INFANT AFFECT EXPRESSIONS

In identifying affect expressions, we took the position that we, the investigators, should make no assumptions about what an infant feels. Instead, we sought those recurring infant behaviors which, in naturalistic circumstances, communicate a definite feeling to a caretaker. These communicated feelings carry information about the condition of the baby and hence serve as an implicit message for action. At any given age, a message should not be idiosyncratic in a single infant and his mother, but should have generality. In effect, we imposed criteria on what behaviors we would consider "affective." These criteria may seem stringent, but we believe they have been useful for research in an area which is easily clouded by bias and uncertainty.

As our work progressed, we became increasingly more concerned with problems of process, of organized complexity, and levels of organization. As a result of what we were willing to call "affective," our attention became focused on three apparent, successive "levels" of development of affect expressions during the first year. A guide to our thinking has been the general systems approach as formulated by Bertalanffy (1968a, 1968b). The general systems approach is interdisciplinary, and offers the promise of integrating different levels of knowledge from diverse sources into a logical interpenetrating body. In biology, it is the direct extension of the organismic approach discussed in our opening chapter. It deals with "systems," where there are problems of interaction of multi-

ple variables of organization, regulation, and goal directed-
ness. For these reasons, we have hopes for its usefulness in our
further work on the development of affect expressions. We not
only need to relate subsequent levels of organization to earlier
ones, to discover how later affect expressions differentiate
from earlier ones—as the work of Bridges (1933) posed the
problem some time ago—we also need to relate research
findings from different levels of inquiry (see Chapter 14). The
general systems approach points to many gaps in our knowledge of relationships (Boulding, 1956). It is too early to
construct a coherent developmental theory of affect organization. Our remarks which follow might be thought of as similar to a sketch of a dimly perceived landscape.

VIEWPOINT

It seems useful to think of the first level of organization as
characteristic of the neonatal period. After this, reorganiza-
tions of behavior occur, with new affect behaviors central to
new communication systems. The new affect behaviors undoubtedly have an innate basis: they appear to be universal;
they emerge at the same developmental points and with the
same initial qualities in congenitally blind infants (Fraiberg,
1971), and twin studies show a more precise concordance of
onset among monozygotic than among dizygotic twins (Freedman, 1965). Since these affect expressions reflect a maturational self-organizing tendency that has come about through
evolution, we speculate that they have some survival value.
From a physiological point of view, the survival value consists
of a built-in message system geared to arouse a caretaker
about urgent needs. From a psychological point of view, the
survival value consists of a facilitation of attachment bonds.

First level: From the point of view of what is communicated
to adults, crying is the only clear affect expression during the
first two months. The infant is either crying or "contented,"

the latter referring to a condition of quiescence or sleep. The
infant's main task is to survive. Both behavior and physiology
seem centered on consolidating homeostatic regulatory systems in the period following birth. Crying seems designed to
ensure survival through communication of conditions of biological need. As we have seen, it communicates a peremptory
message: "Come and change things." Crying operates in a
binary manner: it stops if the mother makes the appropriate
change and continues if she makes the wrong change. Thus
crying also serves to facilitate an adaptive "tuning in" of the
caretaker to the rhythms of needs of the specific young infant.
From the infant's side, it facilitates beginning behavioral
accommodations to the specific environment in the sense of
Piaget (1936) and Sander (1964). Crying also ensures survival
through facilitating attachment bonds in the mother. The
early postpartum presence of the mother, responding to her
infant and actively taking care of his needs, has been shown to
be of crucial importance for the establishment of maternal
affection by the recent work of Klaus, Kennell, and their co-
workers (1970, 1972). The clear importance of crying for
attachment has been discussed by Bowlby (1958, 1969). Our research on unexplained fussiness during this time gives further
emphasis to this point of view. Crying may be so important to
ensuring maternal attachment that its propensity is built into
the young infant even at times when life-threatening physiological needs are not present.

Second level: Further differentiation takes place. Smiling is
added to the crying-quiescence system. The system is no
longer binary. Now there is a surge in the active, curious,
exploratory tendency of the infant. Smiling invites play and a
different type of interaction with the adult when the baby is
awake. Smiling seems designed to enhance attachment
through a different mode. The mother experiences her continuing presence and activity as pleasurable in its own right.
She does not *have* to be there, as in the case of crying, but she
has the feeling that "being with" gives mutual pleasure. From

the researcher's point of view, the infant's behavior is less easily encompassed by any closed system formulation. Smiling denotes the extent to which he is increasingly and actively engaging his environment. Whereas, earlier, regular smiling during wakefulness might have lulled the caretaker into a false sense of security about needs being met, might even have given a mixed, confusing message, now the mother "knows" her infant. She knows his rhythms, his particular needs and how he expresses them. Further, the infant's regulatory systems have become more stable. They are not only more predictable but also more capable of delay, and hence of modification by experience. Now learning takes a leap forward. Smiling propels a positive feedback between the infant and others, so that wakefulness is enhanced and his world expands. The infant now begins a more active process of "tuning in" to his special mother.

Third level: Stranger distress is the new affect expression of the next level. But we speculate beyond the phenomenon itself. Now, in addition to crying-quiescence and smiling, there is fearfulness. The infant communicates that he is fearful upon the approach of a stranger. He does this not only by the expression of fearfulness itself, but by the temporal sequence of its unfolding. As a stranger approaches, he looks with an expression of interest which then becomes one of sober perplexity. This is followed by what is rated as a fearful expression, with frowning and then crying. But, most compelling, the latter part of this response is accompanied by gaze aversion and a turning away of the head and body.

The attachment bond from the mother's side is further reinforced by the specificity of this response to her. Of equal consequence is that the attachment bond from the infant is now specific: no one else will do if there is a separation. Transactions between mother and infant have differentiated to the point where both are "tuned in" to a mutually specific attachment, along with a mutual psychophysiological dependence.

It is noteworthy that the stranger distress response is new in three formal respects: first, unlike earlier affect expressions, it has a motivational characteristic for the infant, not just for the caretaker. The expression does not tell the caretaker what to do so much as it portends action by the infant himself, namely, a withdrawal. Second, the response now seems to be biphasic. There is an initial phase of evaluation and a subsequent phase of intensified affective response leading to action. Third, there appears to be a phasic shift in psychophysiology, at least as indicated by the heart-rate response. The anticipatory cardiac acceleration does not occur earlier in development; we believe it is now an accompaniment of the fearful response and is a manifestation of a major organismic shift. In fact, both behavioral and heart-rate responses, as outlined in the previous chapter, can be divided into two phases. We believe this two-phase affective response sequence is similar to what occurs in adult emotional responses as discussed by Arnold (1970) from the point of view of cognitive psychology and by Pribram (1970) from the point of view of neurophysiology.

Levels beyond: In all of this we have not yet reached the level of representational thought, of language or of symbolic meaning. We have been forced, because of what is possible in research, to focus on affective organization as a biological message system. As psychiatric clinicians and as psychoanalysts, we are usually much more interested in the private or experiential aspects of affective organization. Obviously, these become accessible to investigation only after language development. After that, the growth of the self-system (Mead, 1934; Kohut, 1971), the sense of efficacy (R. White, 1963), and the occurrence of a variety of internalizations (Schafer, 1968) become of increasing importance in affective organization. After that, the human enters into the symbolic universe, and what the child can tell us in his own words opens new fields for research.

14

BIOBEHAVIORAL SHIFTS

In the previous chapter, we advanced a point of view about affect expressions which emphasized their being part of a biological message system. As the infant grows older, these expressions differentiate in the direction of increasing levels of complexity, as measured by what is communicated to the mother and family. But to what extent are there corresponding organismic shifts in the infant? It is now time to resume our discussion of discontinuities and continuities in terms of propositions we derived from the genetic field theory. After reviewing our research data, can we say that our perspective is changed?

The Genetic Field Theory Revisited

We set out on our research enterprise convinced that the genetic field theory would provide a promising and useful orientation. Our findings now permit a reassessment of the propositions from the theory.

1. There Are Uneven Rates of Behavioral and Physiological Development in Infancy

That development proceeds at uneven rates seems incontrovertible when our data from the spheres of sleep, wakefulness, the EEG, and affect expressions are added to the exponentially expanding scientific literature from developmental psychology and neurophysiology. Our research directs attention to two periods of rapid change and two "plateaus" during the first year. The periods of rapid change are: an early postnatal period (from birth to around two and a half months) and a later midyear period (from around five to nine months). Each period is followed by a plateau, or a time during which incremental change is not as prominent. Our research also directs attention to the lack of invariant sequences among different sectors of development within a given infant. Different sectors appear to develop at different rates, although there does seem to be a clustering of changes at certain times.

2. AFFECT BEHAVIORS ARE PROMINENT INDICATORS OF TIMES OF RAPID CHANGE

The genetic field theory pointed to the onset of regular smiling in response to the nodding face, and to the onset of distress in response to the approaching stranger, as correlates of these times of rapid change. Our research findings are consistent with the over-all proposition. However, certain modifications seem appropriate.

First, it was an unexpected finding of our research that a period of increasing wakefulness heralded the onset of the social smile, and that such a period also heralded the onset of stranger distress. These two affect expressions, as dramatic as they were, generally occurred at the end of times of increasing wakefulness, at two and a half to three months and at seven to nine months respectively. Second, each of these affect expressions had developmental antecedents. Early endogenous smiling and early exogenous smiling preceded social smiling; sobering preceded stranger distress. One might speculate that the affect behaviors of social smiling and stranger distress tend to mark the culmination of other underlying changes. Such a view would be bolstered by our findings of EEG shifts also beginning earlier than these behaviors. Thus the changes marked by these affect behaviors might be new qualities resulting from a bringing into synchrony or regulation of a number of different, evenly developing sectors. One must bear in mind the possibility that qualitative change does not necessarily depend upon an over-all rapid rate of development.

3. IN THE DETERMINATION OF BEHAVIOR, THE PROPORTIONAL INFLUENCES OF MATURATION VERSUS EXPERIENCE WILL SHIFT DEMONSTRABLY DURING THE FIRST YEAR

This assertion has a great deal of face validity based on the well-known increasing cognitive capacities of the developing infant. On the other hand, a rigorous test of this proposition would require a specific strategy from behavioral genetics, such as studying identical versus fraternal twins as Freedman has done (1965). Certainly our data do not contradict the proposition. The fact that there is more individual variability during the second time of rapid change than during the first may indeed reflect the increasing influence of a varied environment.

4. EACH TIME OF RAPID CHANGE WILL REFLECT A MAJOR DEVELOPMENTAL SHIFT TO A NEW LEVEL OF ORGANIZATION; THIS SHOULD BE MANIFEST BY THE EMERGENCE OF NOVEL FUNCTIONS IN THE INFANT'S BEHAVIORAL WORLD

We conclude that the evidence seems reasonably convincing for two major biobehavioral shifts in development. Both were seen to occur during the first postnatal year, in terms of the variables we studied, and both are supported by studies from a variety of other disciplines (reviewed in Chapters 1, 8, and 11). Evidence for a first shift between two and three months is now established on the level of behavior (perceptual development, learning development, affective development, and waking development) as well as on the level of neurophysiology (sleep state development, EEG development, and autonomic responsiveness). There is also evidence suggestive of anatomical correlations. Evidence for a second shift between seven and nine months is less extensive. Fewer studies have been done beyond early infancy, but behavioral changes (wakefulness development, affect expression development) and neurophysiological changes (EEG, heart-rate responsiveness) do show a clustering during this age period.

But do these shifts represent major changes in developmental organization? We think they do. Both shifts had dramatic social implications in terms of what the new affect expressions communicated within families. Parents were emphatic about new qualities, and there was an apparent shift in family social organization. At three months, their infants were more human; they were wholly engaging, seemingly eager and curious in a way they had not been before. At seven to nine months, infants were able to communicate that they were attached to a specific person; they were more discriminating about their human wants. When a stranger approached him, a nine-month-old infant was likely to look, to evaluate, and to protest. The message was clear to his mother: she was needed in a way she had not been before; her baby was seen to need her help; no one else would do.

Shifts in qualities are now becoming equally apparent to researchers. Dittrichova and Lapackova (1964) commented about a decade ago that at three months wakefulness seems to be used in a new way. Their speculations about a necessary CNS organizational shift are now supported by data showing the emergence of EEG sleep spindles, shifts in sleep state physiology, shifts in basic learning capacities, shifts in cardiac responsiveness, and by data from a growing number of animal experiments. At seven to nine months, new phenomena of hypersynchronous drowsy activity and K-complexes emerge on the EEG, and, like spindle activity, they remain for the life span. Although heart-rate responsiveness also shows a major organizational shift, our over-all knowledge about a hypothesized shift in CNS organization at this age awaits further studies for substantive support.

The Notion of Biobehavioral Shifts; Mechanisms and Surface-to-Core Relationships

Would the same periods of rapid change be seen from a different perspective? Perhaps not. Our focus on affect expressions certainly biased our field of vision. But numerous measures used in a wide variety of studies do suggest a convergence of findings that support the existence of two major biobehavioral shifts during the first year of postnatal development. Future research must be extended to encompass the social meaning of these shifts within the naturalistic context of the family. There is a need for systematic studies of affect communication systems from the point of view of the developing infant as well as of his transactional world. What messages are given by his affect expressions at different ages? How clear, how efficient, are these messages? How much of any message is universal? How much is related to his particular experience within his family? We are now engaged in a project to answer some of the questions on this level of inquiry. Future research must also focus on microscopic and submicroscopic levels, to look at cellular significance as well as social significance. We must understand more about basic cellular, biochemical, and genetic mechanisms underlying such shifts. We are encouraged by the fact that a number of projects in these areas are being vigorously pursued by others.

But what about the links between such micromechanisms and these organismic shifts at the more global biobehavioral level? Our research already indicates that simple mechanistic interpretations of such changes may be hazardous and incomplete, if not totally inaccurate. This seems true for two reasons. First, mechanisms of behavior may change with new levels of biological organization; formulations which will predict behavior in the newborn will differ fundamentally from those which will predict behavior in the two- or three-month-old (see Chapter 8). Even the "laws" of learning will appear to shift between the two ages. Second, the principles of transformation from one level of organization to the next in this developmental process are unknown. Thus, as one watches babies in a longitudinal study, some behaviors under scrutiny may disappear (such as transitory reflexes or smiling in response to multiple stimuli), others may disappear only to reappear again later (such as thumb-sucking), others may persist but serve different functions at different ages (such as crying at one month and crying in response to a stranger at eight months), while still other early behaviors may correlate with later diverse, even opposite, kinds of behaviors (such as high-intensity reactiveness in the newborn and low-intensity reactiveness in the preschool period as measured by Bell, Weller, and Waldrop [1971]). Perhaps a knowledge of CNS and molecular mechanisms underlying these shifts will result in a set of precise rules which can both explain and predict rates, directions, and sequences of such changes. Perhaps "discontinuities" are only apparent, due to our momentary state of scientific ignorance. Perhaps they await the discovery of what is truly fundamental and continuous. But there is another possibility.

This other possibility forced itself upon us as we pondered what seemed a puzzling, disappointing, and at times monotonously repetitive finding. The very strategy of longitudinal research is geared to elucidating necessary sequences of variables and their correlates within individual cases over time. Our study was no exception. We expected to find invariant sequences during times of rapid change — sequences of emergence for EEG phenomena, cognitive phenomena, and affect expressions. The mapping of such sequences, we thought, could provide a major step toward our developing hypotheses about governing mechanisms. Our findings were otherwise. Although there was evidence for a general clustering of changes, there was no evidence for invariant sequences. Rank order correlations across cases, ordered according to time of onset of individual variables, were consistently low.

Again and again, gross inspection of our data highlighted the same unequivocal conclusion: in virtually all proposed sequences that we could imagine, one or more variables could be found grossly out of sequence in individual cases. We were left with the conundrum of understanding how we could have a cluster of dramatic changes within a limited time period without necessary sequences. Then it dawned upon us.

The organizing mechanism for any major shift would have to be one embedded in the central nervous system. Whether due to a "critical mass" effect (Spitz, 1972) of gradually accumulating quantitative changes or the opening of entirely new channels, whether due to enhancement of already existing simple information flow systems or the addition of higher centers of integration, such a mechanism would not be isolated nor would it be at the surface of the brain. It would probably be at the core of a diffuse network of feedback circuits, necessarily located along the recticular-diencephalic-forebrain axis. Thus surface changes emanating from it, be they reflected in the scalp EEG, affect behaviors, or cognitive skills, would not necessarily be all-or-none in terms of their appearance, nor would their development be fixed in order. In fact, *by definition,* in any field theory, organismic change would not be characterized by linear sequences of cause and effect. In a "field shift," EEG changes would not be expected always to precede or determine affect behaviors. Rather, our findings would be the expected ones: a cluster of changes without invariant sequences. Because of our mechanistic bias, it took us a while to "discover" this in our data. This view, however, is clearly implicit in the developmental theory of Werner (1948), in the psychoanalytic field approaches of Spitz (1959) and French (1941), and, recently, in the neurophysiological theorizing of Bergstrom (1969) and in the sweeping review of the perinatal risk literature by Sameroff and Chandler (1975). Figure 13 schematically represents the alternative predictions which would derive from mechanistic and field explanations of developmental shifts. A core change in the central nervous system is represented by A. B, C, D, and X could represent reflected changes in EEG, cognitive skills, affect behaviors, motor coordinations, and so on. A linear, necessary sequence would be predicted by the first scheme but not by the second.

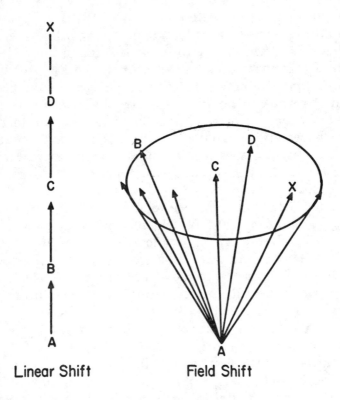

Linear Shift   Field Shift

FIGURE 13

PART IV

WHERE ARE WE NOW?

15

IMPLICATIONS

A. DOWN'S SYNDROME STUDY

An as-yet-unstated hypothesis which has emerged from our study is that the biobehavioral shifts we have been discussing are regulated by maturational factors. These shifts occurred in all the infants studied, and, so far as we could tell, did not require practice or any particular kind of environmental stimulation for their appearance. A definitive test of the maturational hypothesis would require a study of identical and fraternal twins, with attention to concordant and discordant experiences and their outcome. This would be an expansion of the approach already used by Freedman (1965). However, another approach, that of studying mentally retarded infants, also offers the possibility of illuminating findings. Field theory would predict that, in a maturationally determined biobehavioral shift, some aspects of the field could not be distorted without affecting other aspects. In conditions of cognitive retardation, a general synchrony should be preserved. Such a strategy, using mentally retarded children for answering basic questions of this kind, would not be entirely new. Lenneberg (1967), for example, argued that data showing the presence among the retarded of developmental synchrony between motor and language milestones offered cogent evidence for the maturational regulation of language acquisition.

In our future research, we plan to conduct a longitudinal study of a group of Down's syndrome infants (trisomy-21). These infants present a form of genetically determined general retardation which can provide an "experiment in nature." They are now identifiable at birth through chromosomal diagnosis as well as physical diagnosis, and they are known to manifest developmental retardation when tested later in infancy. In other terms, they will predictably evidence a distortion of the cognitive aspect of the developmental field. There is already some evidence that affect expressions and EEG development are also distorted in these infants (Ellingson et al., 1970, 1973; Petre-Quadens, 1966, 1972), but comparative rates of development of different sectors are unknown. We will compare our longitudinal findings about the Down's syndrome infants with those about normal infants reported in this monograph, to see if there are comparable shifts in the areas of cognitive, EEG, and affect expression development. Since cognitive development is slower, a field theory of biobehavioral shifts would predict that the other sectors are also slower. If, on the other hand, the clustering of changes seen in our normal infants does not represent a field shift, if there is not a maturationally determined propensity for general synchrony, then there should be no clustering of changes in the Down's syndrome infants.

B. SOCIAL COMMUNICATION STUDY

On repeated occasions during our research we were bothered by the following question: How do we know that the infant's behavior under scrutiny is affective? The preverbal infant cannot use words to describe how he feels; we cannot gain entry into his private world of experience . . . or can we? We certainly do not feel ourselves completely foreign to his world: when he smiles or frowns, laughs or cries, we are flooded with intuitive responses, affective ones, to which we can give words. But there is a serious scientific risk in describing infant "affects" in terms of our own systems of sensing, experiencing, and understanding. As Spitz pointed out long ago, "adultomorphizing" has led to unwarranted inferences and even gross misrepresentations in developmental psychology. This has been a scientific cul-de-sac not unfamiliar to American behaviorism and psychoanalysis.

As the reader is probably aware, in this monograph we have tried to maintain a conservative stance in drawing inferences about the infant's private experiential world. Our intention has been to keep our descriptive terms and concepts operational, anchored in behavior and physiology. But in our search for meaning, in our urge for continuity with what is felt by the adult, we have repeatedly found ourselves relying on a social level of behavioral observation for orientation. Once we started paying attention to this level, we realized its crucial importance for what is considered affective. If the developing baby did not undergo two major shifts in what was communicated to his family at the same time as the two biobehavioral shifts, there would be much less to interest us. When parents spoke of an emotional change in their baby, we felt comfortable in using terms similar to the ones they used; we could state their contextual origins, and maintain our scientific operationalism. Furthermore, what was communicated to the parents resulted in definite feelings in them, which very often had immediate action consequences. For us, a scientific advantage stemmed from the fact that the affect communications were not only describable by the parental recipients of the message, they were also often susceptible to immediate correction if misinterpreted. This kind of verification resulted from rapid feedback loops in such communication networks: crying could become intense, or smiling could stop. That such rapid self-correcting mechanisms were built into some of these communication networks seemed to underscore their biological importance for survival. Indeed, as we continued to think about this, it seemed that this level of analysis should logically be an orienting point for all research concerned with emotional development in infancy. How the infant communicates and what he communicates, especially in the absence of language, is very often an emotional matter. Biologically based, such affect communications will have a significant role in determining the social context within which the infant develops. Systematic study of such communication systems could yield solid data for a meaningful classification and understanding of early emotional development.

When we realized this, we were surprised to find that there has been practically no research in this area. Three recent books (Ekman, Friesen, and Ellsworth, 1972; Dittmann, 1972; Izard, 1971) have provided major reviews of research related to emotional communication. Practically all research has been done with adults, and serious methodological and conceptual problems have hampered progress until recent times. Only one study, that of Sherman (1927a, 1927b), has been done on infants, and it was not a longitudinal study. Because of this gap in our knowledge, we have immersed ourselves in a study of the development of affect communications during infancy. We are making longitudinal observations on a small group of normal infants in the context of their families, using a variety of interviewing and filming techniques. Our intention is to obtain as much naturalistic information as we can from mothers and fathers about what is communicated by specific filmed behaviors. This information will form the basis for subsequent rating scales that we will construct and use in one or more separate experimental studies, which will also make use of our original visual materials.

OTHER TIMES OF BIOBEHAVIORAL SHIFT; IMPLICATIONS FOR DISEASE PATHOGENESIS

There is abundant evidence that the two biobehavioral shifts we have described in infancy are not the only ones that occur in childhood. The period from about the middle of the second year of postnatal life until its end has emerged as another time of major shift. Spitz (1959), in his genetic field theory, has conceptualized this as a time of rapid change. It is marked by the onset of the "no gesture" and represents a fundamental watershed, not only in language acquisition but also in the development of the child's autonomy and hence his whole sphere of social relations (Spitz, 1957). This period is also a pivotal one for developmental change in Piaget's (1936, 1937, 1945) view, for it contains within it a shift from sensori-motor intelligence to representational intelligence, where evocative memory is possible and mental inventions can be made beyond immediate experience. Lenneberg (1967) discusses the sudden increase in vocabulary size at this age, and cites its independence from cultural and environmental context. He also summarizes other data which lead him to conclude that this period is one in which there is a maturationally determined state of readiness for language acquisition.

The period from five to seven years is still another time of major shift. Sheldon White (1965) has masterfully summarized changes in learning, perception, cognitive style, speech usage, and general intelligence which take place during this period. In addition, there is an onset of right-left discrimination and a marked enhancement of the ability to locate and discriminate objects in space. Before this period, the findings from children's learning experiments resemble those from similar experiments on animals; after this period, the findings resemble more those from experiments on human adults. White concludes that this marks a basic change from "juvenile mental processes" to "higher mental processes," and that there is, from then on, a hierarchical arrangement between the two. The more juvenile level becomes inhibited, but is potentially available to influence behavior according to a more primitive or associative mode. White states: "Perhaps the 5-7 period is a time when some maturational development, combining perhaps with influences in the modal environment, inhibits a broad spectrum of first-level function in favor of a new, higher level of function" (p. 213).

The similarity of these ideas to those enduring conceptualizations of Hughlings Jackson (1884) and of Freud (1905) is striking. Hughlings Jackson's doctrine of progressive "evolution" of function during development and "dissolution" during later neuropathology has provided a useful model for almost a century of clinicians and researchers (see documentation by Lassek, 1970). According to Hughlings Jackson, symptoms of disease have both negative and positive elements, resulting from loss of higher function on the one hand and release of lower functions on the other. Freud's theory of psychosexual development included an emphasis on early pregenital stages, which retain an organization but become inhibited, especially around five to seven years; it is then that superego formation is prominent and latency is entered. Further, the biobehavioral shift around the end of the second year, mentioned above, corresponds to the anal stage of psychosexual development.

The reader may ask: What is the point of all this? Of what practical consequence are these shifts in childhood? Is this not just an artistic perspective on development or, at best, a highly abstract, theoretical approach? Some mention of applications may help dispel some of these doubts.

First, these periods of biobehavioral shift may represent times of vulnerability. The developing child may be more susceptible to psychological and physiological stress at these times. Regulatory mechanisms, which themselves are undergoing change, may be distorted or overrun. At a recent workshop on neurophysiological factors associated with the sudden infant death syndrome (Weitzman and Graziani, 1972), such a hypothesis was advanced to account for this tragic disorder. Sudden infant death syndrome (SIDS), which affects about 10,000 infants per year in the United States, refers to the sudden death of a previously healthy infant, usually when he had been thought to be peacefully asleep. The peak age incidence is from two to three months, precisely at the time of the first biobehavioral shift we have outlined. Its occurrence during sleep makes us recall the massive changes that take place in sleep physiology as part of this shift. The hypothesis advanced by the workshop (of which the senior author was a member) was that SIDS infants represent an exaggeration of what is usually "a normal time of instability," and that respiratory regulation is interfered with, resulting in a prolonged and lethal apnea. Although brief apneic episodes occur normally during REM sleep, certain predisposing factors may combine to cause longer apnea and death during a critical period of brain growth at two to three months—a time when there may be an imbalance of inhibitory systems. The predisposing factors may include an innate functional abnormality of the respiratory centers in the lower brain stem, mild viral infections, and sleep deprivation. Current research at a number of centers is aimed at testing this multifactorial hypothesis. Although it is beyond the scope of this monograph, a review of epidemiological studies seems indicated to see if other disorders are concentrated at the times of biobehavioral shift we have outlined. We suspect a number of these will be found.

A second application of recognizing biobehavioral field shifts has to do with longitudinal research. Longitudinal studies of personality development, of which quite a few were continuously active during the 30's, 40's, and 50's (see Kagan, 1964), were uniformly disappointed in not finding antecedent nonintelligence personality variables in early childhood which predicted later personality variables in either childhood or adulthood (Mischel, 1969). From our current vantage point of seeing a number of biobehavioral field shifts, we have no reason to be surprised. As discussed above, biobehavioral field shifts imply changes of regulatory systems toward greater complexity. From the point of view of behavior, they introduce discontinuities. Furthermore, at the present state of our knowledge, the laws of transformation from one level of organization to another are unknown. These considerations are important for a new wave of long-range longitudinal studies which are now being carried out following recent advances in behavioral genetics. Most of these studies are being done on populations identified as being at genetic risk for schizophrenia, but one envisions similar studies on populations at genetic risk for other major psychiatric disorders. The research strategy is geared to observing significant factors in the pathogenesis of disease *in statu nascendi*. An additional hope is to identify antecedents which can serve as early biological or psychological "markers" for purposes of intervention. Clearly, if the researcher expects to follow antecedent variables of consequence through biobehavioral shifts, he must focus on these particular times to observe the vicissitudes of the variables of interest.

BIOBEHAVIORAL SHIFTS AND THERAPEUTIC RECONSTRUCTION

As already mentioned, long-term longitudinal studies have often been unsuccessful in finding continuities in normal personality development. As clinicians, we might ask: Why is that so difficult? We find historical continuities easily in our patients; we often can "trace the red thread backwards." In fact, allowing the patient to feel a sense of historical continuity about himself is therapeutic (Erikson, 1964). Why is it, then, that we cannot predict continuity in development?

The answer lies in a twofold consideration of the difference between historical reconstruction and development itself. The first consideration can be expressed in linear terms. Looking backward, it is easy to follow the "red thread" from the more complex to the less complex; once we know the result, it is easy to trace continuities through a multiplicity of antecedent factors and see which ones are relevant to that result. Looking forward, however, is an impossible task. How can we predict, other than in gross probabilistic terms, developmental pathways as they will be affected by countless future environmental contingencies, much less "the thousand natural shocks that flesh is heir to"? Even knowing these events, how can we predict which will weigh heavily and which will be of little consequence? This consideration, although often ignored, has been stated before, for example, by Freud (1920), by A. Freud (1966), and by Lorenz (personal communication). It is represented in Figure 14. Knowing E, one can get to A, but knowing only A, one has only a small chance of getting to E.

The second consideration arises from this monograph. We have learned that it is not sufficient to think of development in terms of linear sequences. Biobehavioral field shifts occur. During them, there is qualitative change with structural reorganization. It is not just that developmental lines are shifted; there is an active process going on, during which new modes of being emerge. The idea of new modes, or formulae,

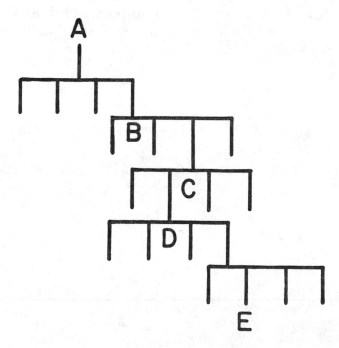

FIGURE 14

being discovered at certain times of development is an important aspect of the epigenetic theories of both Spitz (1959; Spitz, Emde, and Metcalf, 1970) and Erikson (1950). Development is not merely a passive, deterministic resultant of genes and environment, it is an active, interactive, and *creative* process. This is especially apparent at times of biobehavioral shifts. If we were to superimpose this perspective on our previous diagram of linear development, we might have arrows shifting the lines at certain junctures so as to cause movement in a variety of novel directions.

It is no surprise, then, that there is a disparity between tracing forward through child observation and tracing backward through analytic reconstruction, between analysis and synthesis, as Freud put it (1920). The restructuring of memory by subsequent experience and the issues involved in veridical versus schematic memory are discussed elsewhere (for example, Kris, 1956; Wolff, 1967). Our point here is to illustrate that a knowledge of biobehavioral field shifts should contribute to any such discussion.

APPENDIX

Sleep NREM

Eyes closed; face appears relaxed; no REMs.

Sleep REM

Eyes closed; REMs are seen under eyelids; occasional transient (1 sec.) eyelid opening during large upward-rolling eye movements.

Drowsy NREM

Eyes appear "glassy" and are open for more than 30 seconds of a 1-minute observation; occassional to frequent eyelid blinking; face immobile; no REMs.

Drowsy REM

Same criteria as for drowsy NREM except REMs are seen and facial expression often is fixed with a "strain-ed," wide-eyed appearance.

Sucking NREM

At least half of a 1-minute observation involves sucking; no REMs.

Sucking REM

Same as sucking NREM except REMs are seen during sucking as well as during pauses.

Fussy-Awake

Expiratory whimpers occurring more than three times but occupying less than 10 seconds of a 1-minute observation.

Fussy REM

Same criteria as for fussy-awake except REMs are seen under closed eyelids. This state usually interrupts an ongoing sleep-REM state.

Crying-Awake

Expiratory whimpers and/or overt crying for more than 10 seconds of a 1-minute observation.

Crying REM

Same criteria as for crying-awake except REMs are seen under closed eyelids. This state usually interrupts an ongoing fussy-REM or sleep-REM state.

Alert-Inactive

Less movement; eyes are "bright"; eyes pursue a slow-moving object for a brief period.

Alert-Active

During the 1-minute observation, there is gross movement of two extremities, or of one extremity with much head movement.

TABLE B
INTENSITY RATING SCALES FROM INTERVIEW DATA

Fussiness

Fussiness is defined as a state of irritability not clearly related to physiological needs such as hunger or specific externally caused pain (e.g., doctor's shot). Its behavioral manifestations include crying, restlessness, muscular tension, or an inability to relax and fall asleep.

Rating Scale

0 = Fussiness (as defined above) absent for a 24-hour period; appropriate fussing is present.
1 = Intermittent or mild crying for 5-10 minutes or tensing of bodily musculature and restlessness for 10-20 minutes.
2 = Intermittent crying or restlessness for several short periods or one period lasting less than an hour. (The difference between 1 and 2 ratings is mainly frequency and duration.)
3 = Hard crying or extreme restlessness sometimes including stiffening for periods of approximately an hour. Hard crying for at least 1/2 hour. (The difference between 2 and 3 is mainly intensity.)
4 = Hard crying or extreme restlessness for periods longer than an hour.
5 = No alert state in a 24-hour period without fussiness.

Separation Distress

0 = Absent
1 = Irregular but only when tired or in stressful circumstances such as being in a strange environment or being hungry. This rating is for minimal distress with pronounced frowning or minimal or brief fussing. It includes an "equivocal" rating.
2 = Irregular but occurs in alert states in addition to when tired, though only after a period of time has elapsed after the mother leaves. There is mild to moderate distress with fussing and/or whimpering.
3 = Usually occurs in alert states immediately following separation; there is moderate to marked distress with fussing and crying, but as is true of the lower ratings, it is easily soothed by the mother's return or it diminishes within 5 minutes without her return.
4 = Also usually occurs in alert states immediately after separation. However, in this category distress is marked and prolonged. It requires more than the mother's presence for soothing or it does not diminish within 5 minutes without her return.

Stranger Distress

0 = Absent
1 = Irregular and only when tired, or in unusually stressful circumstances (rough handling, strange environment); minimal distress (frown or fearful expression, brief fussing). This includes an "equivocal" rating.
2 = Irregular, but occurs in alert states only with stranger picking up infant or intruding vigorously. This includes mild to moderate distress with fussing and whimpering. The infant is easily soothed by the mother's presence with a rapid warming up to the stranger.
3 = Usually occurs in alert states upon visual approach. There is moderate to marked distress with fussing and crying. The infant is easily soothed by the mother, however, and there is relatively rapid warming to strangers.
4 = Usually occurs in alert states with visual or auditory approach. Distress is marked, prolonged, and requires more than the mother's presence for soothing without easy warming to strangers.

TABLE C
SOCIAL SMILING SCALE

Rating   *Criteria*

1 = *None.* No social smiling.

2 = *Minimal.* Minimal evidence for social smiling; fleeting or minimal smiles seen on one or two occasions only during alert states (might be seen by one observer only).

3 = *Irregular.* Clear and full social smiles (bilateral upturning of the corners of the mouth for more than 1 second). These occur in response to the human face. However, usually the voice is necessary to elicit a smile and the tester has some difficulty in eliciting it and has the impression that he "has to work at it." The smile occurs relatively infrequently.

4 = *Predictable.* Smiling is a predictable social response to the human face. It is a full smile which occurs with high frequency. Sometimes this rating includes a ready smile in response to the face where the voice is also necessary for its predictable elicitation.

TABLE D
PRIMARY FILM RATING SCALE — SOCIAL-INTERACTION SERIES

I. *Intensity of discrimination of mother compared to unfamiliar person.* (Responses may be more intense and with quicker smiling, more over-all bodily activity, "eyes brightening," etc.). This item rated during first three months only.
    A. _____No difference in responsiveness
        _____Slight difference in responsiveness
        _____Major difference in responsiveness
    B. _____Response and direction
    Comments:

II. *Separation distress*
    Global Impression:_____Present (pronounced frowning, whimpering, crying, or following)
                    _____Absent
    A. Facial
        _____No change
        _____Blank expression
        _____Sober; studious
        _____Frown
        _____Whimpering
        _____Overt cry
    B. Motor
        _____Increased activity
        _____No change
        _____Decreased activity
        _____Immobile
    C.   Specific searching after the mother
        _____None
        _____Visual searching in direction the mother exited
        _____Physical effort to follow the mother after she leaves
    Comments:

III. *Recovery from separation distress* (graded according to a 3-point scale)
    _____Does not apply
    _____Relatively complete recovery during 1 minute
    _____Beginning of recovery in 1 minute with intervention, but not complete
    _____Recovery only when mother intervenes
        _____Looking at mother is sufficient (with or without voice)
        _____Mother must hold
        _____Persistence beyond initial intervention
        _____Several minutes more but mother soothes completely
        _____Mood lasts beyond mother's intervention
    Comments:

IV. *Stranger distress with the mother absent.* (In each of the following categories rate the response to each of the following stimuli.)

F = Looking at silent face
V = In response to voice which is added to visual stimulation
P = In response to being picked up
(If smiling occurs with any of these responses, denote by "sm.")
Global Impression: _____Present (pronounced frowning, whimpering, crying, or following)
_____Absent

A. Facial
_____Initial smiling
_____No change
_____Fascinated
_____Sober;studious
_____Frown or fearful
_____Whimper or brief fussing
_____Overt cry

B. Motor
_____Increased activity
_____No change
_____Decreased activity
_____Immobile

C. Direction of response
_____Turning toward (either by looking or active interaction)
_____Turning toward and then away (ambivalent response)
_____Avoidance

Comments:

V. *Recovery from stranger distress* (rated according to following grading scale)
_____Does not apply
_____Beginning of recovery with stranger but not complete
_____Recovery only when mother intervenes
_____Looking at the mother is enough (with or without voice)
_____Mother needs to hold for recovery
_____Persistence of distress beyond the mother's initial intervention
_____Several minutes more, but the mother soothes completely
_____Mood lasts beyond the mother's intervention

Comments:

VI. *Response to the stranger after the mother's intervention*
A. _____Unchanged
_____Increased interest without smiling
_____Increased interest with smiling
_____No signs of increased interest in the stranger
B. Compares faces
_____Yes _____No

Comments:

VII. *Stranger distress with the mother present.* This scale is the same as stranger distress with the mother absent (IV).

VIII. *Recovery from stranger distress with the mother present* (same as item V).

Table E
Intensity Scales for Film Rating

Separation Distress Intensity		Stranger Distress Intensity	
Facial Expression:	*Points Awarded*	*Facial Expression:*	*Points Awarded*
Blank-fascinated	0	Fascinated	+1
Sober-studious	1	Sober-studious	0
Frown-fearful	2	Frown-fearful	−1
Whimper-fuss	3	Whimper-fuss	−2
Overt cry	4	Overt cry	−3
Searching:		*Direction:*	
No searching	0	Toward	+1
Visual searching	1	Toward & away (ambiv.)	0
Physical effort to follow	2	Avoidance	−1

Note: Separation distress intensity was obtained by adding the points awarded for facial expression and searching (max. = 6). Stranger distress intensity was obtained by adding the points awarded for facial expression and direction of the visual gaze for each phase of approach; that is, silent approach, vocalization, and pick-up (max. = −4 for each phase and −12 for total sequence).

TABLE F
RELIABILITY SUMMARY FROM FILM RATINGS

Item	Reliability %	Item	Reliability %
I. Discrimination of mother	76	V. Rate of Recovery	92%
II. Separation Distress		VI. Stranger response after	
Global impression	97)	mother returns	
Facial expression	79)	Interest	83)
Motor	74)	Compares faces	84)
Search after mother	90)	Combined	83%
Combined	85%	VII. Stranger Distress with	
III. Rate of Recovery	97%	mother present	
IV. Stranger Distress with		Global impression	90
mother absent		Facial expression	
Global impression	95	Nodding face	70)
Facial expression		Voice added	74)
Nodding face	76)	Pick-up	78)
Voice added	62)	Combined	73%
Pick-up	64)	Motor	
Combined	69%	Nodding face	63)
Motor		Voice added	64)
Nodding face	71)	Pick-up	64)
Voice added	62)	Combined	64%
Pick-up	64)	Direction of Response	
Combined	65%	Nodding face	79)
Direction		Voice added	80)
Nodding face	85)	Pick-up	78)
Voice added	87)	Combined	79%
Pick-up	78)	VIII. Rate of Recovery	90%
Combined	83%		

TABLE G
RELIABILITY STUDY FROM INTERVIEW DATA CATEGORIES
ILLUSTRATING THE EXTENT TO WHICH TWO JUDGES AGREE ON AN ITEM
AS PRESENT

Major Categories	Agreement on Subcategories	Total Agreement
Teething	Eleven of 12 tooth eruptions were agreed upon. Twelve of 12 fussiness symptoms were agreed upon and 21 of 24 coded associated symptoms were agreed upon (there were 5 sub subcategories of these including gumming, chewing, diarrhea, fever, and nighttime awakening).	91.7%
Illnesses	Twenty-one of 24 specific subcategories were agreed upon by the two judges in terms of the nature of the illness and onset within one week.	87.5%
Feeding changes	Six out of 6 agreements occurred on weaning events (with 4 sub subcategories here), 5 out of 7 agreements occurred on items of feeding disturbances and their onset.	84.6%
Stress events	Sixteen of 20 agreements occurred for 3 subcategories of stress events, namely family moves, visits, and unusual events.	80%

Note: Negative agreements were not counted, as they would artificially inflate the reliability estimates.

TABLE H

HOURS OF DAYTIME SLEEP, NIGHTTIME SLEEP, AND MEAN LONGEST WAKE PERIOD

Longitudinal Study of the First Year

Age in Months	X̄ Day Sleep (6 a.m. to 6 p.m.)	S.D.	X̄ Night Sleep (6 p.m. to 6 a.m.)	S.D.	Ratio of Night/Day	X̄ Longest Wake Period	S.D.
1	6.61	1.61	8.98	1.24	1.36	4.0	1.91
2	6.13	1.53	9.22	0.86	1.50	5.0	2.93
3	5.91	1.96	9.52	1.08	1.61	5.01	3.06
4	5.33	1.72	10.22	0.86	1.92	4.22	2.19
5	4.91	1.63	10.33	0.99	2.10	4.62	2.58
6	4.95	1.49	10.00	1.12	2.02	4.1	1.91
7	4.38	1.05	9.90	0.93	3.26	4.25	1.54
8	4.30	1.07	9.85	1.04	2.29	4.83	.80
9	4.20	1.07	9.98	0.83	2.38	4.02	.95
10	4.68	1.22	10.10	0.80	2.16	4.07	.54
11	4.22	0.95	10.04	0.65	2.38	4.74	1.13
12	4.29	0.75	10.08	0.69	2.35	5.08	2.33

TABLE I
MEAN VALUES OF STATES FOR NORMAL NEWBORN STUDIES
1967-1972
(Values expressed as % of observation time)

N	20	20	7	30	30
Technique of observation	Behavioral-naturalistic	Polygraph	Behavioral-naturalistic	Behavioral-naturalistic	Behavioral-naturalistic
When observed	a.m. & p.m., feed. to feed.	10 p.m. to 8 a.m.	day & night	a.m. & p.m., feed. to feed.	a.m. to p.m. feed. to feed.
Age	1 & 2 days	24 hours	1 day	1 & 2 days	1 & 2 days
Sleep-REM	45.70	49.50	47.82	46.08	47.95
Sleep-NREM	20.85	21.26	19.98	20.60	18.91
Drowsy*	5.90	5.89	7.83	8.27	8.11
Fussy &** crying	11.94	10.51**	14.73	11.27	10.25
Awake*	8.84	6.28	5.89	6.64	7.72
Sucking*	6.75	6.54	3.68	6.61	7.05
Basetime	218.20 min.	10 hours	12 hours	212.2 min.	232.8 min.

*These states are subdivided according to the system described in Table A and mean values of subgroups are available
**Includes artifact time

TABLE J
SLEEP SPINDLE RATING SYSTEM
(From Metcalf, 1970)

Frequency:	12-14 Hz.
Grade I:	Variation of ± 1 Hz within a single burst.
Grade II:	Occasional variations of ± 0.5 Hz within a single burst.
Amplitude:	Grade I: 7-10/uv. Grade II: 25-30/uv.
Duration:	Grade I: 0.4-1.0 sec. Grade II: 1-3 sec.; rarely 3-5 sec.
Modulation:	Grade I: not fusiform. Grade II: fusiform.
Scalp locus:	Maximally developed prevertex often shifting between hemispheres, occasionally bilaterally symmetrical. Grade I: Vertex only. Grade II. Vertex dominant. May occur simultaneously in anterior temporal regions.

TABLE K
RATING SYSTEM — K-COMPLEXES

A. Individuation. The degree to which a K-complex is readily differentiated from background EEG activity. Individuation describes the development of a consistent and predictable "full morphology" of the K-complex as noted by Roth, Shaw, and Green (1956). Rating: percent of individuated K-complexes. Scores of 0, 1, 2, 3, and 4 were assigned for 0-5%, 5-25%, 25-50%, 50-75%, and 75-100%, respectively.

B. Vertex focus. The degree to which the scalp vertex voltage dominance of the K-complex is evident. Rating: percent of K-complexes which have a vertex focus. Scores of 0, 1, 2, 3, and 4 were assigned for the same percentages as the individuation scores.

C. Repetition. Frequency with which the initial prominent, sharp, high-amplitude wave of the K-complex is seen. To be classed as "repetitive" the sharp wave must have more than three phases preceding the following slow wave. Rating: percent of repetitive K-complexes in a record. Scores of 0, 1, 2, 3, and 4 were assigned for 95-100%, 75-95%, 50-75%, 25-50%, and 0-25%, respectively.

D. Spread. Proportion of K-complexes which record simultaneously in high central and in lateral regions (frontotemporal and/or temporal-temporal). Rating: percent of spreading K-complexes. Scores of 0, 1, 2, 3, and 4 were assigned for the same percentages as the repetition scores.

A score for the entire record was attained by averaging the sum of the ratings for each parameter; i.e., Grade = (A + B + C + D)/4.

TABLE L
HYPERSYNCHRONOUS DROWSY ACTIVITY RATING SCALE
(D. R. Metcalf, M.D.)

A Rating of	0	=	No hypersynchronous drowsy activity
A Rating of	1	=	1- to 2-second brief bursts of such activity
A Rating of	2	=	Prolonged bursts
A Rating of	3	=	Long continuous runs

TABLE M
NUMBER OF CASES SHOWING STRANGER DISTRESS BY MONTHS

N = 14 possible cases each month

Months

	5	6	7	8	9	10	11	12
Stranger #1	1	4	5	6	8	7	8	9
Stranger #2	0	4	3	5	6	6	6	9

REFERENCES

Agnew, H., Webb, W., & Williams, R. (1966), The First Night Effect: An EEG Study of Sleep. *Pyschophysiol.*, 2:263-266.

Ainsworth, M. (1967), *Infancy in Uganda.* Baltimore: John Hopkins Press.

——— , Salter, D., & Wittig, B. A. (1969), Attachment and Exploratory Behavior of One-Year-Olds in a Strange Situation. In: *Determinants of Infant Behaviour,* ed. B. M. Foss, 4:111-136. New York: Wiley.

Altman, J. (1967), Postnatal Growth and Differentiation of the Mammalian Brain, with Implications for a Morphological Theory of Memory. In: *The Neurosciences,* ed. G. C. Quarton, T. Melnechuk, & F. O. Schmitt. New York: Rockefeller University Press, pp. 723-743.

Amacher, P. (1965), Freud's Neurological Education and Its Influence on Psychoanalytic Theory. *Psychol. Issues,* Monogr. No. 16. New York: International Universities Press.

Ambrose, A. (1961), The Development of the Smiling Response in Early Infancy. In: *Determinants of Infant Behaviour,* ed. B. M. Foss, 1:179-201. New York: Wiley.

———(1963), The Age of Onset of Ambivalence in Early Infancy: Indications from the Study of Laughing. *J. Child Psychol. & Psychiat.,* 4:167-181.

Anders, T., Emde, R., & Parmelee, A., eds. (1971), *A Manual of Standardized Terminology, Techniques and Criteria for Scoring of States of Sleep and Wakefulness in Newborn Infants.* UCLA Brain Information Service, NINDS Neurological Information Network.

——— & Hoffman, E. (1973), The Sleep Polygram: A Potentially Useful Tool for Clinical Assessment in Human Infants. *Amer. J. Ment. Deficiency,* 77:506-514.

——— & Roffwarg, H. (1973), The Effects of Selective Interruption and Deprivation of Sleep in the Human Newborn. *Develop. Psychobiol.,* 6:77-89.

——— & Zangen, M. (1972), Sleep State Scoring in Human Infants. *Psychophysiol.,* 9:653-654.

Arnold, M. G. (1970), Perennial Problems in the Field of Emotion. In: *Feelings and Emotion, the Loyola Symposium,* ed. M. B. Arnold. New York: Academic Press, pp. 169-185.

Aserinsky, E., & Kleitman, N. (1955), A Motility Cycle in Sleeping Infants as Manifested by Ocular and Gross Bodily Activity. *J. App. Physiol.,* 8:11-18.

Ausubel, D. P., & Sullivan, E. (1970), *Theory and Problems of Child Development,* 2nd ed. New York: Grune & Stratton.

179

Baldwin, J. M. (1895), *Mental Development in the Child and in the Race.* New York: Macmillan.

Bayley, N. (1932), A Study of the Crying of Infants during Mental and Physical Tests. *J. Gen. Psychol.,* 40:306-329.

——(1969), *Bayley Scales of Infant Development.* New York: The Psychological Corporation.

Bekoff, M., & Fox, M. (1972), Postnatal Neural Ontogeny: Environment-Dependent and/or Environment-Expectant. *Develop. Psychobiol.,* 5:323-341.

Bell, R. Q., Weller, G. M., & Waldrop, M. F. (1971), Newborn and Preschooler: Organization of Behavior and Relations between Periods. *Monogr. Soc. Res. Child Develop.,* 36: Nos. 1-2, Serial No. 142.

Bell, S. (1970), The Development of the Concept of Object as Related to Infant-Mother Attachment. *Child Develop.,* 41:291-311.

—— & Ainsworth, M. (1972), Infant Crying and Maternal Responsiveness. *Child Develop.,* 43:1171-1190.

Benjamin, J. (1965), Developmental Biology and Psychoanalysis. In: *Psychoanalysis and Current Biological Thought,* ed. N. Greenfield & W. Lewis. Madison: University of Wisconsin Press, pp. 57-80.

Berger, H. (1929), Über das Elektrenkephalogram des Menschen. *Arch. Psychiat. Nervenk.,* 87:527-570.

Bergman, T., Haith, M., & Mann, L. (1971), Development of Eye Contact and Facial Scanning in Infants. Paper presented at the SRCD Convention, Minneapolis, April.

Bergstrom, R. M. (1969), Electrical Parameters of the Brain during Ontogeny. In: *Brain and Early Behavior,* ed. R. J. Robinson. London: Academic Press, pp. 15-41.

Bernfeld, S. (1944), Freud's Earliest Theories and the School of Helmholtz. *Psychoanal. Quart.,* 13:341-362.

Bernstein, P., Emde, R. N., & Campos, J. J. (1973), Wakefulness and Feeding in Human Newborns. *Psychosom. Med.,* 35:322-329.

Bernstein, S. & Mason, W. A. (1962), The Effects of Age and Stimulus Condition on the Emotional Response of Rhesus Monkeys: Responses to Complex Stimuli. *J. Gen. Psychol.,* 101:279-298.

Bertalanffy, L. von (1934), *Modern Theories of Development.* New York: Harper Torchbooks, 1962.

——(1952), *Problems of Life.* New York: Harper Torchbooks, 1960.

——(1967), *Robots, Men and Minds: Psychology in the Modern World.* New York: Braziller.

——(1968a), *General System Theory, Foundations, Development, Applications.* New York: Braziller, 1969.

——(1968b), *Organismic Psychology and Systems Theory.* Barre, Mass.: Clark University Press with Barre Publishers.

Bijou, S. W., & Baer, M. D. (1961), *Child Development,* Vol. 1. *A Systematic and Empirical Theory.* New York: Appleton-Century-Crofts.

—— ——(1965), *Child Development,* Vol. 2. *Universal State of Infancy.* New York: Appleton-Century-Crofts.

Bond, E. L. (1972), Perception of Form by the Human Infant. *Psychol. Bull.* 77:225-245.

Boulding, K. (1956), General Systems Theory—The Skeleton of Science. *Management Science,* 2:197-208.

Bowlby, J. (1958), The Nature of the Child's Tie to His Mother. *Internat. J. Psycho-Anal.,* 39:350-373.

——(1969), *Attachment and Loss,* Vol. 1. New York: Basic Books.

————(1973), *Attachment and Loss,* Vol. 2. New York: Basic Books.
Brackbill, Y. (1958), Extinction of the Smiling Response in Infants as a Function of Reinforcement. *Child Develop.,* 29:115-124.
————(1962), Research and Clinical Work with Children. In: *Some Views on Soviet Psychology.* Washington, D.C.: American Psychological Association.
Brazelton, T. B. (1962), Crying in Infancy. *Pediatrics,* 29:579-588.
Brennan, W. M., Ames, E. W., & Moore, R. W. (1966), Age Differences in Infant's Attention to Patterns of Different Complexities. *Science,* 151:354-356.
Bridges, K. M. B. (1933), Emotional Development in Early Infancy. *Child Develop.,* 3:324-341.
Bronshtein, A. I., & Petrova, E. P. (1952), The Auditory Analyzer in Young Infants. In: *Behavior in Early Infancy,* ed. Y. Brackbill & G. C. Thompson. New York: Free Press, 1967.
Buhler, C. (1930), *The First Year of Life.* New York: Day.
———— & Hetzer, H. (1935), *Testing Children's Development from Birth to School Age.* New York: Farrar & Rinehart.
Bühler, K. (1918), *Die Geistige Entwicklung des Kindes,* 4th ed. Jena: Fischer, 1924.
Burns, P., Sander, L., Stechler, G., & Julia, H. (1972), Distress in Feeding: Short-Term Effects of Caretaker Environment of the First 10 Days. *J. Amer. Acad. Child Psychiat.,* 11:427-439.
Caldwell, B., & Hersher, L. (1964), Mother-Infant Interaction during the First Year of Life. *Merrill-Palmer Quart.,* 10:119-128.
Campos, J. J., Emde, R., Gaensbauer, T., Sorce, J., & Henderson, C. (1975), Cardiac Behavioral Interrelations in the Reactions of Infants to Strangers. *Devel. Psychol.,* 11:589-601.
Caton, R. (1875), The Electric Currents of the Brain. *Brit. Med. J.,* 2:278.
Cattell, P. (1940), *The Measurement of Intelligence in Infants and Young Children,* rev. ed. New York: The Psychological Corporation, Johnson Reprint Corp., 1960.
Chase, M. H. (1970), The Digastric Reflex in the Kitten and Adult Cat: Paradoxical Amplitude Fluctuations during Sleep and Wakefulness. *Arch. Ital. Biol.,* 108:403-422.
————(1971), Brain Stem Somatic Reflex Activity in Neonatal Kittens during Sleep and Wakefulness. *Physiol. & Behav.,* 7:165-172.
———— (1972), Patterns of Reflex Excitability during the Ontogenesis of Sleep and Wakefulness. In: *Sleep and the Maturing Nervous System,* ed. C. Clemente, D. P. Purpura, & F. Mayer. New York: Academic Press, pp. 253-285.
———— (1973), Somatic Reflex Activity during Sleep and Wakefulness. In: *Basic Sleep Mechanisms,* ed. O. Petre-Quadens & J. Schlag. New York: Academic Press.
———— & Sterman, M. (1967), Maturation of Patterns of Sleep and Wakefulness in the Kitten. *Brain Res.,* 5:319-329.
————, Stern, W., & Walter, P., eds. (1972), *Sleep Research,* Vol. 1. Brain Information Service/Brain Research Institute, Los Angeles: University of California at Los Angeles.
———— ———— , eds. (1973), *Sleep Research,* Vol. 2. Brain Information Service/Brain Research Institute, Los Angeles: University of California at Los Angeles.
Cohen, J. (1965), Some Statistical Issues in Psychological Research. In: *The Handbook of Clinical Psychology,* ed. B. B. Wolman. New York: McGraw-Hill, pp. 95-121.

Collard, R. (1967), Fear of Strangers and Play Behavior in Kittens with Varied Social Experience. *Child Develop.*, 38:877-899.

Conel, J. L. (1941), *The Postnatal Development of the Human Cerebral Cortex*, Vol. 2. *The Cortex of the One-Month Infant.* Cambridge, Mass.: Harvard University Press.

———(1947), *The Postnatal Development of the Human Cerebral Cortex*, Vol. 3. *The Cortex of the Three-Month Infant.* Cambridge, Mass.: Harvard University Press.

Corman, H. H., & Escalona, S. K. (1969), Stages of Sensorimotor Development: A Replication Study. *Merrill-Palmer Quart.*, 15:351-361.

Dearborn, G. V. N. (1910), *Motor-Sensory Development: Observations on the First Three Years of a Child.* Baltimore, Md.: Warwick & York.

Décarie, T. Gouin (1962), *Intelligence and Affectivity in Early Childhood.* New York: International Universities Press, 1965.

———(1974), *The Infant's Reaction to Strangers.* New York: International Universities Press.

Denisova, M., & Figurin, N. (1929), The Question of the First Associated Appetitional Reflexes in Infants. *Vopr. Genet. Refleksol. Pedol. Mladen*, 1:81-88.

Dittmann, A. T. (1972), *Interpersonal Messages of Emotion.* New York: Springer.

Dittrichova, J., & Lapackova, V. (1964), Development of the Waking State in Young Infants. *Child Develop.*, 35:365-370.

Drage, J. S., Kennedy, C., Berendes, H., Schwarz, B. K., & Weiss, W. (1966), The Apgar Score as an Index of Infant Morbidity. *Develop. Med. Child Neurol.*, 8:141-148.

Dreyfus-Brisac, C. (1966), The Bioelectric Development of the Central Nervous System during Early Life. In: *Human Development*, ed. F. Faulkner. Philadelphia: Saunders.

——— (1970), Ontogenesis of Human Sleep in Human Prematures after 32 Weeks of Conceptual Age. *Develop. Psychobiol.*, 3:91-121.

Ekman, P., Friesen, W. V., & Ellsworth, P. (1972), *Emotion in the Human Face: Guidelines for Research and an Integration of Findings.* Elmsford, N.Y.: Pergamon Press.

Ellingson, R. J., Eisen, J. D., & Ottersberg, G. (1973), Clinical Electroencephalographic Observations on Institutionalized Mongoloids Confirmed by Karyotype. *Electroencephal. Clin. Neurophysiol.*, 34:193-196.

——— , Menolascino, F. J., & Eisen, J. D. (1970), Clinical EEG Relationships in Mongoloids Confirmed by Karyotype. *Amer. J. Ment. Defic.*, 74:645-650.

Emde, R. N., & Harmon, R. (1972), Endogenous and Exogenous Smiling Systems in Early Infancy. *J. Amer. Acad. Child. Psychiat.*, 11:177-200.

——— & Koenig, K. (1969a), Neonatal Smiling and Rapid Eye Movement States. *J. Amer. Acad. Child Psychiat.*, 8:57-67.

——— ——— (1969b), Neonatal Smiling, Frowning, and Rapid Eye Movement States: II. Sleep-Cycle Study. *J. Amer. Acad. Child Psychiat.*, 8:637-656.

———, McCartney, R., & Harmon, R. (1971), Neonatal Smiling in REM States: IV. Premature Study. *Child Develop.*, 42:1657-1661.

——— & Metcalf, D. R. (1970), An Electroencephalographic Study of Behavioral Rapid Eye Movement States in the Human Newborn. *J. Nerv. Ment. Dis.*, 150:376-386.

——— Swedberg, J. & Suzuki, B. (1975), Human Wakefulness and Biological Rhythms during the First Postnatal Hours. *Arch. Gen. Psychiat.*, 35:780-783.

Erikson, E. H. (1950), *Childhood and Society*. New York: Norton.
―――― (1964), *Insight and Responsibility: Lectures on the Ethical Implications of Psychoanalytic Insight*. New York: Norton.
Escalona, S. (1953), Emotional Development in the First Year of Life. In: *Problems of Infancy and Childhood*, ed. M. Senn. New York: Josiah Macy, Jr. Foundation, pp. 11-92.
―――― (1968), *The Roots of Individuality*. Chicago: Aldine.
Fantz, R. (1961), A Method for Studying Depth Perception in Infants under Six Months of Age. *Psychol. Rec.*, 11:27-32.
―――― (1964), Visual Experience in Infants: Decreased Attention to Familiar Patterns Relative to Novel Ones. *Science*, 146:668-670.
Fraiberg, S. (1969), Libidinal Object Constancy and Mental Representation. *The Psychoanalytic Study of the Child*, 24:9-47. New York: International Universities Press.
―――― (1971), Smiling and Stranger Reaction in Blind Infants. In: *Exceptional Infant*, Vol. 2. *Studies in Abnormalities*, ed. J. Hellmuth. New York: Brunner/Mazel, pp. 110-127.
Freedman, D. G. (1961), The Infant's Fear of Strangers and the Flight Response. *J. Child Psychol. & Psychiat.*, 2:242-248.
―――― (1965), Hereditary Control of Early Social Behaviour. In: *Determinants of Infant Behaviour*, ed. B. M. Foss, 3:149-159. New York: Wiley.
―――― (1971), Genetic Influences on Development of Behavior. In: *Normal and Abnormal Development of Behavior*, ed. G. B. A. Stoelinga & J. J. Van der Werff Ten Bosch. Leiden: Leiden University Press.
――――, King, J. A., & Elliot, O. (1961), Critical Period in the Social Development of Dogs. *Science*, 133:1016-1017.
French, T. (1941), Goal, Mechanism, and Integrative Field. I. A Biological Problem. *Psychosom. Med.*, 3:226-252. Also in: *Psychoanalytic Interpretations, The Selected Papers of Thomas M. French* (1970), Chicago: Quadrangle, pp. 160-197.
Freud, A. (1936), *The Ego and the Mechanisms of Defense*. New York: International Universities Press, 1946.
―――― (1966), Links between Hartmann's Ego Psychology and the Child Analyst's Thinking. In: *Psychoanalysis: A General Psychology*, ed. R. Loewenstein, L. Newman, M. Schur, & A. Solnit. New York: International Universities Press, pp. 16-27.
Freud, S. (1900), The Interpretation of Dreams. *Standard Edition*, 4 & 5. London: Hogarth Press, 1953.
―――― (1905), Three Essays on the Theory of Sexuality. *Standard Edition*, 7:123-243. London: Hogarth Press, 1953.
―――― (1911), Formulations on the Two Principles of Mental Functioning. *Standard Edition*, 12:218-226. London: Hogarth Press, 1958.
―――― (1920), The Psychogenesis of a Case of Homosexuality in a Woman. *Standard Edition*, 18:147-172. London: Hogarth Press, 1955.
―――― (1926), Inhibitions, Symptoms and Anxiety. *Standard Edition*, 20:87-172. London: Hogarth Press, 1961.
Gaensbauer, T., & Emde, R. N. (1973), Wakefulness and Feeding in Human Newborns. *Arch. Gen. Psychiat.*, 28:894-897.
Gesell, A., & Ames, L. B. (1937), Early Evidence of Individuality in the Human Infant. *Sci. Mon.*, 45:217-225.
―――― & Ilg, F. L. (1943), *Infant and Child in the Culture of Today*. New York: Harper.

Gewirtz, J. L. (1965), The Course of Infant Smiling in Four Child-Rearing Communities in Israel. In: *Determinants of Infant Behaviour,* ed. B. M. Foss, 3:205-248. New York: Wiley.

Globus, G. (1966), Rapid Eye Movement Cycle in Real Time. *Arch. Gen. Psychiat.,* 15:654-659.

Goldstein, K. (1939), *The Organism.* New York: American Book Company.

Graham, F., & Clifton, R. K. (1966), Heart-Rate Change as a Component of the Orienting Response. *Psychol. Bull.,* 65:305-320.

———— & Jackson, J. (1970), Arousal Systems and Infant Heart-Rate Responses. In: *Advances in Child Development and Behavior,* ed. H. W. Reese & L. P. Lipsitt, 5:60-111. New York: Academic Press.

Gratch, G., & Landers, W. F. (1971), Stage IV of Piaget's Theory of Infant's Object Concepts: A Longitudinal Study. *Child Develop.,* 42:359-372.

Greenberg, N. H. (1965), Developmental Effects of Stimulation during Early Infancy: Some Conceptual and Methodological Considerations. *Ann. N.Y. Acad. Sci.,* 118:831-859.

Greenough, D. (1973), Environmental Effects on Brain Anatomy. Paper presented at Winter Conference on Brain Research, Vail, Colorado, January.

Grossman, W. I., & Simon, B. (1969), Anthropomorphism: Motive, Meaning, and Causality in Psychoanalytic Theory. *The Psychoanalytic Study of the Child,* 24:78-111. New York: International Universities Press.

Haith, M. (1969), Infrared Television Recording and Measurement of Ocular Behavior in the Human Infant. *Amer. Psychol.,* 24:279-285.

———— (1973), Visual Scanning in Infants. In: *The Competent Infant: A Handbook of Readings.* New York: Basic Books, pp. 320-323.

———— (1976), Visual Competence in Early Infancy. In: *Handbook of Sensory Physiology,* 8, ed. R. Held, H. Leibowitz, & H. L. Teuber. New York: Springer.

Harmon, R. J., & Emde, R. N. (1972), Spontaneous REM behaviors in a Microcephalic Infant. *Percept. & Motor Skills,* 34:827-833.

Hartmann, H. (1939), *Ego Psychology and the Problem of Adaptation.* New York: International Universities Press.

Haynes, H., White, B. L., & Held, R. (1965), Visual Accommodation in Human Infants. *Science,* 148:528-530.

Hebb, D. O., & Reisen, A. H. (1943), The Genesis of Irrational Fears. *Bull. Canad. Psychol. Assn.,* 3:49-50.

Hellbrügge, T. (1960), The Development of Circadian Rhythms in Infants. *Cold Spring Harbor Symp. Quant. Biol.,* 25:311-323.

Hendrick, I. (1934), *Facts and Theories of Psychoanalysis,* 2nd ed. New York: Knopf, 1939.

Hess, E. H. (1959), Two Conditions Limiting the Critical Age for Imprinting. *J. Comp. Physiol. Psychol.,* 52:515-518.

Hoff, H. E., & Breckenridge, C. G. (1954), Intrinsic Mechanisms in Periodic Breathing. *AMA Arch. Neur. Psychiat.,* 72:11-42.

Holt, R. R. (1965), A Review of Some of Freud's Biological Assumptions and Their Influence on His Theories. In: *Psychoanalysis and Current Biological Thought,* ed. N. S. Greenfield & W. C. Lewis. Madison: University of Wisconsin Press, pp. 93-124.

————, ed. (1967), Motives and Thought: Psychoanalytic Essays in Honor of David Rapaport. *Psychol. Issues,* Monogr. No. 18/19. New York: International Universities Press.

Hruska, K., & Yonas, A. (1972), Developmental Changes in Cardiac Responses to the Optical Stimulus of Impending Collision, *Psychophysiol.*, 9:272.

Hughlings Jackson, J. (1884), Evolution and Dissolution of the Nervous System. *Selected Writings of John Hughlings Jackson*, Vol. 2, ed. J. Taylor. New York: Basic Books, 1958, pp. 45-75.

Hull, C. L. (1952), *A Behavior System*. New Haven: Yale University Press.

Hunt, J. M. (1965), Intrinsic Motivation and Its Role in Psychological Development. In: *Nebraska Symposium on Motivation, 1965*, ed. D. Levine. Lincoln: University of Nebraska Press, pp. 189-282.

Hutt, S. J., Lenard, H. G., & Prechtl, H. F. R. (1969), Psychophysiological Studies in Newborn Infants. In: *Advances in Child Development and Behavior*, ed. L. P. Lipsitt & H. W. Reese, 4:127-172. New York: Academic Press.

Izard, C. (1971), *The Face of Emotion*. New York: Meredith.

Jackson, J. C., Kantowitz, S., & Graham, F. (1971), Can Newborns Show Orienting? *Child Develop.*, 42:107-120.

Jacobsen, C. F., Jacobsen, M. M., & Yoshioka, J. G. (1932), Development of an Infant Chimpanzee during Her First Year. *Comp. Psychol. Monogr.*, 9(1).

Jeffrey, W. E., & Cohen, L. B. (1971), Habituation in the Human Infant. In: *Advances in Child Development and Behavior*, ed. H. W. Reese, 6:63-97. New York: Academic Press.

Johnson, L. C. (1973), Are Stages of Sleep Related to Waking Behavior? *Amer. Sci.* 61:326-338.

——— & Karpen, W. E. (1968), Autonomic Correlates of the Spontaneous K-Complex. *Psychophysiol.*, 4:444-449.

Jones, M. C. (1926), The Development of Early Behavior Patterns in Young Children. *Pediat. Sem.*, 33:537-585.

Jouvet-Mounier, D., Astic, L., & Lacote, D. (1970), Ontogenesis of the States of Sleep in Rat, Cat and Guinea Pig during the First Postnatal Month. *Develop. Psychobiol.*, 2:216-239.

Kagan, J. (1964), American Longitudinal Research on Psychological Development. *Child Develop.*, 34:1-32.

——— (1970), Attention and Psychological Change in the Young Child. *Science*, 170:826-832.

——— (1971), *Change and Continuity in Infancy*. New York: Wiley.

——— & Moss, H. A. (1962), *Birth to Maturity*. New York: Wiley.

Kasatkin, N. I. (1969), The Origin and Development of Conditioned Reflexes in Early Childhood. In: *Handbook of Contemporary Soviet Psychology*, ed. M. Cole & I. Maltzman. New York: Basic Books, pp. 71-85.

Kearsley, R. B. (1973), The Newborn's Response to Auditory Stimulation: A Demonstration of Orienting and Defensive Behavior. *Child Develop.*, 44:582-590.

Kessen, W., Haith, M., & Salapatek, P. H. (1970), Human Infancy: A Bibliography and Guide. In: *Carmichael's Manual of Child Psychology*, Vol. 1, 3rd ed., ed. H. Mussen. New York: Wiley, pp. 287-445.

Kiloh, L. G., McComas, A. J., & Osselton, J. W. (1972), *Clinical Electroencephalography*, 3rd ed. New York: Appleton-Century-Crofts.

King, D. L. (1966), A Review and Interpretation of Some Aspects of the Infant-Mother Relationship in Mammals and Birds. *Psychol. Bull.*, 65:143-155.

Klaus, M. H., Jerauld, R., Kreger, N. C., McAlpine, W., Steffa, M., & Kennell, J. H. (1972), Maternal Attachment, Importance of the First Post-Partum Days. *New Eng. J. Med.*, 286:460-463.

———, Kennell, J. H., Plumb, N., & Zuehlke, S. (1970), Human Maternal Behavior at the First Contact with her Young. *Pediat.*, 46:187-192.

Klein, G. S. (1969), Freud's Two Theories of Sexuality. In: *Clinical-Cognitive Psychology: Models and Integrations*, ed. L. Breger. Englewood Cliffs, N.J.: Prentice-Hall, pp. 136-181.

Kleitman, N. (1939), *Sleep and Wakefulness.* Chicago: University of Chicago Press.

——— (1963), *Sleep and Wakefulness*, 2nd ed. Chicago: University of Chicago Press.

——— & Engelmann, T. G. (1953), Sleep Characteristics of Infants. *J. Appl. Physiol.*, 6:269-282.

Kligman, D., Smyrl, R., & Emde, R. (1975), A "Nonintrusive" Longitudinal Study of Infant Sleep. *Psychosom. Med.*, 37:448-453.

Köhler, O. (1954), Das Lächeln als angeborene Ausdrucksbewegung [The Smile as an Innate Facial Expression]. *Z. Menschl. Vererb. & Konstitutionslehre,* 32:390-398.

Kohut, H. (1971), *The Analysis of the Self.* New York: International Universities Press.

Korner, A. (1969), Neonatal Startles, Smiles, Erections, and Reflex Sucks as Related to State, Sex, and Individuality. *Child Develop.*, 40:1039-1053.

Kripke, D. F. (1972), An Ultradian Biologic Rhythm Associated with Perceptual Deprivation and REM Sleep. *Psychosom. Med.*, 34:221-234.

Kris, E. (1956), The Recovery of Childhood Memories in Psychoanalysis. *The Psychoanalytic Study of the Child*, 11:54-88. New York: International Universities Press.

Kron, R. E., Stein, M., Goddard, K. E., & Phoenix, M. D. (1967), Effect of Nutrient upon the Sucking Behavior of Newborn Infants. *Psychosom. Med.*, 29:24-32.

Landers, W. F. (1971), Effects of Differential Experience on Task. *Develop. Psychol.*, 5:48-54.

Langworthy, O. R. (1933), Development of Behavior Patterns and Myelinization of the Nervous System in the Human Fetus and Infant. *Contrib. Embryol.*, 24:3-57.

Lassek, A. M. (1970), *The Unique Legacy of Doctor Hughlings Jackson.* Springfield: Charles C Thomas.

Lenard, H. G. (1970), The Development of Sleep Spindles in the EEG during the First Two Years of Life. *Neuropädiat.*, 1:264-276.

Lenneberg, E. H. (1967), *Biological Foundations of Language.* New York: Wiley.

Lipsitt, L. P. (1967), Learning in the Human Infant. In: *Early Behavior: Comparative and Developmental Approaches*, ed. H. W. Stevenson, H. L. Rheingold, & E. Hess. New York: Wiley, pp. 225-247.

——— & Jacklin, C. (1971), Cardiac Deceleration and Its Stability in Human Newborns. *Develop. Psychol.*, 5:535.

——— & Kaye, H. (1965), Change in Neonatal Response to Optimizing and Nonoptimizing Sucking Stimulation. *Psychonom. Sci.*, 2:221-222.

Livingston, R. B. (1967), Brain Circuitry Relating to Complex Behavior. In: *The Neurosciences*, ed. G. C. Quarton, T. Melnechuk, & F. O. Schmitt. New York: Rockefeller University Press, pp. 568-577.

Loewald, H. W. (1960), On the Therapeutic Action of Psycho-Analysis, *Internat. J. Psycho-Anal.*, 41:16-33.

——— (1970), Psychoanalytic Theory and the Psychoanalytic Process. *The Psychoanalytic Study of the Child*, 25:45-68. New York: International Universities Press.

Lubchenco, L. O., Hansman, C., & Boyd, E. (1966), Intrauterine Growth in Length and Head Circumference as Estimated from Live Births at Gestational Ages from 26 to 42 Weeks. *Pediat.*, 37:403-408.

———, Searls, D. T., & Brazie, J. V. (1972), Neonatal Mortality Rate: Relationship to Birthweight and Gestational Age. *J. Pediat.*, 81:814-822.

Marler, P., & Hamilton, W. (1966), *Mechanisms of Animal Behavior.* New York: Wiley.

Marquis, D. P. (1931), Can Conditioned Responses Be Established in the Newborn Infant? *J. Genet. Psychol.*, 39:479-492.

McCandless, B. R. (1967), *Children, Behavior and Development,* 2nd ed. New York: Holt, Rinehart & Winston.

McGinty, D. J. (1971), Encephalization and the Neural Control of Sleep. In: *Brain Development and Behavior,* ed. M. B. Sterman, D. J. McGinty, & A. M. Adinolfi. New York: Academic Press, pp. 335-355.

Mead, G. (1934), *Mind, Self and Society,* ed. C. Morris. Chicago: University of Chicago Press.

Metcalf, D. R. (1969), The Effect of Extrauterine Experience on the Ontogenesis of EEG Sleep Spindles. *Psychosom. Med.*, 31:393-399.

——— (1970), EEG Sleep Spindle Ontogenesis. *Neuropädiat.*, 1:428-433.

———, Mondale, J., & Butler, F. (1971), Ontogenesis of Spontaneous K-Complexes. *Psychophysiol.*, 8:340-347.

Miller, D. J., Cohen, L. B., & Hill, K. T. (1970), A Methodological Investigation of Piaget's Theory of Object Concept Development in the Sensory-Motor Period. *J. Exp. Child Psychol.*, 9:59-85.

Miller, G. A., Galanter, E., & Pribram, K. (1960), *Plans and the Structure of Behavior.* New York: Holt.

Mischel, W. (1969), Continuity and Change in Personality. *Amer. Psychol.*, 24:1012-1018.

Moltz, H. (1960), Imprinting: Empirical Basis and Theoretical Significance. *Psychol. Bull.*, 57:291-314.

Montagu, A. (1961), Neonatal and Infant Immaturity in Man. *J. Amer. Med. Assn.*, 178:156-157.

Morgan, G. A., & Ricciuti, H. N. (1969), Infants' Responses to Strangers during the First Year. In: *Determinants of Infant Behaviour,* ed. B. M. Foss, 4:253-272. New York: Wiley.

Munsinger, H. (1971), *Fundamentals of Child Development.* New York: Holt.

Mussen, P. H., ed. (1970), *Carmichael's Manual of Child Psychology,* Vol. 1. New York: Wiley.

———, Conger, J. J., & Kagan, J. (1974), *Child Development and Personality,* 4th ed. New York: Harper & Row.

Needham, J. (1931), *Chemical Embryology.* London: Macmillan.

O'Brien, J. S. (1970), Lipids and Myelination. In: *Developmental Neurology.* Springfield, Ill.: Charles C Thomas, pp. 262-286.

Othmer, E., Hayden, M., & Segelbaum, R. (1969), Encephalic Cycles during Sleep and Wakefulness in Humans: A 24-Hour Pattern. *Science,* 164:447-449.

Paine, R. S. (1965), The Contribution of Developmental Neurology to Child Psychiatry. *J. Amer. Acad. Child Psychiat.*, 4:353-386.

Papousek, H. (1961), Conditioned Head Rotation Reflexes in the First Months of Life. *Acta. Pediat.*, 50:565-576.

——— (1967), Experimental Studies of Appetitional Behavior in Human Newborns and Infants. In: *Early Behavior,* ed. H. W. Stevenson, E. H. Hess, & H. L. Rheingold. New York: Wiley, pp. 249-277.

———— & Bernstein, P. (1969), The Functions of Conditioning Stimulation in Human Neonates and Infants. In: *Stimulation in Early Infancy,* ed. A. Ambrose. New York: Academic Press. pp. 229-252.

Paradise, E. B., & Curcio, F. (1974), The Relationship of Cognitive and Affective Behaviors to Fear of Strangers in Male Infants. *Develop. Psychol.,* 10:476-483.

Paradise, J. (1966), Maternal and Other Factors in the Etiology of Infantile Colic. *JAMA,* 197:191-199.

Paraskevopoulos, J., & Hunt, J. McV. (1971), Construction and Imitation under Different Conditions of Rearing. *J. Gen. Psychol.,* 119:301-321.

Parmelee, A. H., & Michaelis, R. (1971), Neurological Examination of the Newborn. In: *Exceptional Infant,* Vol. 2. *Studies in Abnormalities,* ed. J. Hellmuth. New York: Brunner/Mazel, pp. 3-24.

————, Stern, E., & Harris, M. A. (1972), Maturation of Respiration in Premature and Young Infants. *Neuropädiat.,* 3:294-304.

————, Wenner, W. H., Akiyama, Y., Schultz, M. & Stern, E. (1967), Sleep States in Premature Infants. *Develop. Med. & Child. Neurol.,* 9:70-77.

———— ———— & Schulz, H. R. (1964), Infant Sleep Patterns from Birth to 16 Weeks of Age. *J. Pediat.,* 65:576-582.

Peiper, A. (1963), *Cerebral Function in Infancy and Childhood.* New York: Consultants Bureau.

Peterfreund, E. (1971), Information, Systems, and Psychoanalysis: An Evolutionary Biological Approach to Psychoanalytic Theory. *Psychol. Issues,* Monogr. No. 25/26. New York: International Universities Press.

Petre-Quadens, O. (1966), Paradoxical Sleep and Dreaming in the Mentally Retarded. *J. Neurol. Sci.,* 3:608-612.

———— (1972), Sleep in Mental Retardation. In: *Sleep and the Maturing Nervous System,* ed. C. D. Clemente, D. P. Purpura, & F. E. Mayer. New York: Academic Press, pp. 383-417.

Piaget, J. (1936), *The Origins of Intelligence in Children,* 2nd ed. New York: International Universities Press, 1952.

———— (1937), *The Construction of Reality in the Child.* New York: Basic Books, 1954.

———— (1945), *Play, Dreams and Imitation in Childhood.* New York: Norton, 1962.

Polak, P. R., Emde, R. N., & Spitz, R. A. (1964a), The Smiling Response to the Human Face: I. Methodology, Quantification and Natural History. *J. Nerv. Ment. Dis.,* 139:103-109.

———— ———— ————(1964b), The Smiling Response: II. Visual Discrimination and the Onset of Depth Perception. *J. Nerv. Ment. Dis.,* 139:407-415.

Pomerleau-Malcuit, A., & Clifton, R. K. (1973), Neonatal Heart-Rate Response to Tactile, Auditory and Vestibular Stimulation in Different States. *Child Develop.,* 44:485-496.

Pratt, K. C. (1954), The Neonate. In: *Manual of Child Psychology,* 2nd ed., ed. L. Carmichael. New York: Wiley, pp. 215-291.

Prechtl, H. F. R. (1958), The Directed Head-Turning Response and Allied Movements of the Human Baby. *Behavior,* 13:212-242.

————, Akiyama, Y., Zinkin, P., & Grant, D. K. (1968), Polygraphic Studies of the Fullterm Newborn. I. Technical Aspects and Qualitative Analysis. In: *Studies in Infancy,* ed. M. C. Bax & R. C. McKeith. London: Heinemann, pp 1 21.

Preyer, W. (1888), *The Mind of the Child,* Part II. *The Development of the Intellect.* New York: Appleton.

Pribram, K. (1970), Feelings as Monitors. In: *Feelings and Emotions,* The Loyola Symposium, ed. M. B. Arnold. New York: Academic Press, pp. 41-52.

Rabinowicz, T. (1964), The Cerebral Cortex of the Premature Infant of the 8th Month. In: *Progress in Brain Research,* ed. D. Purpura & J. Schade, 4:39-92. Amsterdam: Elsevier.

Rapaport, D. (1959), The Structure of Psychoanalytic Theory: A Systematizing Attempt. *Psychol. Issues,* Monogr. No. 6. New York: International Universities Press, 1960.

Razran, G. H. S. (1933), Conditioned Responses in Children: A Behavioral and Quantitative Critical Review of Experimental Studies. *Arch. Psychol.,* 24(No. 148).

Rheingold, H. (1969), The Effect of a Strange Environment on the Behavior of Infants. In: *Determinants of Infant Behaviour,* ed. B. M. Foss, 4:137-166. New York: Barnes & Noble.

———— & Eckerman, C. O. (1973), Fear of the Stranger: A Critical Examination. In: *Advances in Child Development and Behavior,* ed. H. W. Reese. New York: Academic Press, pp. 185-222.

————, Gewirtz, J. L., & Ross, H. W. (1959), Social Conditioning of Vocalizations in the Infant. *J. Comp. Physiol. Psychol.,* 52:68-73.

Robson, K., Pedersen, F., & Moss, H. (1969), Developmental Observations of Diadic Gazing in Relation to the Fear of Strangers and Social Approach Behavior. *Child Develop.,* 40:619-627.

Roffwarg, H. P., Muzio, J. N., & Dement, W. C. (1966), Ontogenetic Development of the Human Sleep-Dream Cycle. *Science,* 152:604-619.

Rosenzweig, M. (1973), Effects of Experiments on Rat Brain: A Model for Aspects of Human Development and for Memory Storage? Paper presented to the Winter Conference on Brain Research, Vail, Colorado, January.

————, Krech, D., Bennett, E., & Diamond, M. (1968), Modifying Brain Chemistry and Anatomy by Enrichment or Impoverishment of Experience. In: *Early Experience and Behavior,* ed. G. Newton & S. Levine. Springfield, Ill.: Charles C Thomas, pp. 258-298.

Roth, M., Shaw, J., & Green, J. (1956), The Form, Voltage Distribution and Physiological Significance of the K-Complex. *Electroenceph. & Clin. Neurophysiol.,* 88:385-405.

Sackett, G. (1966), Monkeys Reared in Isolation with Pictures as Visual Input: Evidence for Innate Releasing Mechanism. *Science,* 154:1468-1473.

Sameroff, A. (1971), Can Conditioned Responses Be Established in the Newborn Infant: 1971? *Develop. Psychol.,* 5:1-12.

————, Cashmore, T. F., & Dykes, A. C. (1973), Heart-Rate Deceleration during Visual Fixation in Human Newborns. *Develop. Psychol.,* 8:117-119.

———— & Chandler, M. (1975), Reproductive Risk and the Continuum of Caretaking Casualty. In: *Review of Child Development Research,* ed. F. Horowitz, M. Hetherington, S. Scarr-Salapatek, & G. Siegel, 4. Chicago: University of Chicago Press.

Sander, L. (1962), Issues in Early Mother-Child Interaction. *J. Amer. Acad. Child Psychiat.,* 1:141-166.

———— (1964), Adaptive Relationships in Early Mother-Child Interaction. *J. Amer. Acad. Child Psychiat.,* 3:231-264.

———— (1969), Regulation and Organization in the Early Infant-Caretaker System. In: *Brain and Early Behavior,* ed. R. Robinson. London: Academic Press, pp. 311-332.

———— & Julia, H. L. (1966), Continuous Interactional Monitoring in the Neonate. *Psychosom. Med.,* 28:822-835.

————, Stechler, G., Burns, P., & Julia, H. (1970), Early Mother-Infant Interaction and 24-Hour Patterns of Activity and Sleep. *J. Amer. Acad. Child Psychiat.*, 9:103-123.

Scarr, S., & Salapatek, P. (1970), Patterns of Fear Development during Infancy. *Merrill-Palmer Quart.*, 16:53-90.

Schaefer, E. S., & Bayley, N. (1963), Maternal Behavior, Child Behavior and Their Intercorrelations from Infancy through Adolescence. *Monogr. Soc. Res. Child Develop.*, 28(No. 3).

Schafer, R. (1968), *Aspects of Internalization.* New York: International Universities Press.

Schaffer, H. (1966), The Onset of Fear of Strangers and the Incongruity Hypothesis. *J. Child Psychol. & Psychiat.*, 7:95-106.

———— & Callender, W. (1959), Psychological Effects of Hospitalization in Infancy. *Pediat.*, 24:528-539.

———— & Emerson, P. (1964), The Development of Social Attachments in Infancy. *Monogr. Soc. Res. Child Develop.*, 29(No. 3).

————, Greenwood, A., & Parry, M. (1972), The Onset of Wariness. *Child Develop.*, 43:165-175.

Schulte, F. J., Kaiser, H. J., Engelhart, S., Bell, E. F., Castell, R., & Lenard, H. F. (1973), Sleep Patterns in Hyperphenylalaninema: A Lesson on Seratonin to Be Learned from Phenylketornuria. *Pediat. Res.*, 7:588-599.

Schultz, M. A., Schulte, F. J., Akiyama, Y., & Parmelee, A. H. (1968), Development of Electroencephalographic Sleep Phenomena in Hypothyroid Infants. *Electroencephal. & Clin. Neurophysiol.*, 25:351-358.

Schur, M. (1966), *The Id and the Regulatory Principles of Mental Functioning.* New York: International Universities Press.

Schwartz, A., Campos, J., & Baisel, E. (1973), The Visual Cliff: Cardiac and Behavioral Correlates on the Deep and Shallow Sides at Five and Nine Months of Age. *J. Exper. Child Psychol.*, 15:85-99.

Scott, J. P. (1963), The Process of Primary Socialization in Canine and Human Infants. *Monogr. Soc. Res. Child Develop.*, 28(No. 1).

Sherman, M. (1927a), The Differentiation of Emotional Responses in Infants. I. Judgments of Emotional Responses from Motion Picture Views and from Actual Observation. *J. Comp. Psychol.*, 7:265-285.

———— (1927b), The Differentiation of Emotional Responses in Infants. II. The Ability of Observers to Judge the Emotional Characteristics of the Crying of Infants and of the Voice of an Adult. *J. Comp. Psychol.*, 7:335-351.

Siegel, S. (1956), *Nonparametric Statistics for the Behavioral Sciences,* ed. H. Harlow. New York: McGraw-Hill.

Sluckin, W. (1965), *Imprinting and Early Learning.* London: Methuen.

Spitz, R. (1950), Anxiety in Infancy: A Study of Its Manifestations in the First Year of Life. *Internat. J. Psycho-Anal.*, 31:138-143.

———— (1957), *No and Yes: On the Genesis of Human Communication.* New York: International Universities Press.

———— (1959), *A Genetic Field Theory of Ego Formation.* New York: International Universities Press.

————.(1961), Some Early Prototypes of Ego Defenses. *J. Amer. Psychoanal. Assn.*, 9:626-651.

———— (1965), *The First Year of Life: A Psychoanalytic Study of Normal and Deviant Development of Object Relations.* New York: International Universities Press.

—— (1972), Bridges: On Anticipation, Duration and Meaning. *J. Amer. Psychoanal. Assn.*, 20:721-735.

——, Emde, R., & Metcalf, D. (1970), Further Prototypes of Ego Formation: A Working Paper from a Research Project on Early Development. *The Psychoanalytic Study of the Child*, 25:417-441. New York: International Universities Press.

—— & Wolf, M. (1946), Anaclitic Depression, An Inquiry into the Genesis of Psychiatric Conditions in Early Childhood, II. *The Psychoanalytic Study of the Child*, 2:313-342. New York: International Universities Press.

Stechler, G., & Carpenter, G. (1967), A Viewpoint on Early Affective Development. In: *Exceptional Infant*, Vol. 1. *The Normal Infant*, ed. J. Hellmuth. New York: Brunner/Mazel, pp. 165-189.

Sterman, M., & Clemente, C. (1962), Forebrain Inhibitory Mechanisms: Sleep Patterns Induced by Basal Forebrain Stimulation in the Behaving Cat. *Exper. Neurol.*, 6:102-117.

—— & Hoppenbrouwers, T. (1971), The Development of Sleep-Waking and Rest-Activity Patterns from Fetus to Adult in Man. In: *Brain Development and Behavior*, ed. M. Sterman, D. McGinty, & A. Adinolfi. New York: Academic Press, pp. 203-227.

Stevens, A. (1971), Attachment Behavior, Separation Anxiety, and Stranger Anxiety. In: *The Origins of Human Social Relations*, ed. B. M. Foss. New York: Academic Press, pp. 137-146.

Stewart, A., Weiland, I., Leider, A., Mangham, C., Holmes, T., & Ripley, H. (1954), Excessive Infant Crying (Colic) in Relation to Parent Behavior. *Amer. J. Psychiat.*, 110:687-694.

Stone, L. & Church, J. (1975), *Childhood and Adolescence: A Psychology of the Growing Person*, 3rd ed. New York: Random House.

Tennes, K., Emde, R., Kisley, A., & Metcalf, D. (1972), The Stimulus Barrier in Early Infancy: An Exploration of Some Formulations of John Benjamin. *Psychoanalysis and Contemporary Science*, 1:206-234. New York: Macmillan.

—— & Lampl, E. (1964), Stranger and Separation Anxiety in Infancy. *J. Nerv. Ment. Dis.*, 139:247-254.

Thomas, A., Birch, H. G., Chess, S., Hertzig, M. E., & Korn, S. (1963), *Behavioral Individuality in Early Childhood*. New York: New York University Press.

Thompson, W., & Grusec, J. (1970), Studies of Early Experience. In: *Carmichael's Manual of Child Psychology*, 3rd ed., Vol. 1., ed. P. H. Mussen. New York: Wiley, pp. 565-654.

Wachs, T. P., Uzgiris, I. C., & Hunt, J. McV. (1971), Cognitive Development in Infants of Different Age Levels and from Different Environmental Backgrounds: An Exploratory Investigation. *Merrill-Palmer Quart.*, 17:283-317.

Waddington, C. (1940), *Organizers and Genes*. London: Cambridge University Press.

Watson, J. (1930), *Behaviorism*. Chicago: University of Chicago Press.

—— & Watson, R. (1921), Studies in Infant Psychology. *Sci. Mon.*, 13:493-515.

Weitzman, E., & Graziani, L. (1972), Report on Workshop on Neurophysiologic Factors Associated with Sudden Infant Death Syndrome. NICHD Conference, Washington, D.C., July.

Welker, W. I. (1956), Effects of Age and Experience on Play and Exploration of Young Chimpanzees. *J. Comp. Physiol. Psychol.*, 49:223-226.

Werner, H. (1948), *Comparative Psychology of Mental Development*, rev. ed. New York: International Universities Press, 1957.

———— & Kaplan, B. (1963), *Symbol Formation: An Organismic-Developmental Approach to Language and the Expression of Thought.* New York: Wiley.

Wessel, M., Cobb, J., Jackson, E., Harris, G., & Detwiler, A. (1954), Paroxysmal Fussing in Infancy, Sometimes Called Colic. *Pediat.,* 14:421-434.

Wetherford, M., & Cohen, L. (1973), Developmental Changes in Infant Visual Preferences for Novelty and Familiarity. *Child Develop.,* 44:416-424.

White, R. W. (1963), Ego and Reality in Psychoanalytic Theory. *Psychol. Issues,* Monogr. No. 11. New York: International Universities Press.

White, S. (1965), Evidence for a Hierarchical Arrangement of Learning Processes. In: *Advances in Child Development and Behavior,* ed. L. Lipsitt & C. Spiker, 2:187-220. New York: London: Academic Press.

———— (1970), The National Impact Study of Head Start. In: *Disadvantaged Child,* Vol. 3, ed. J. Hellmuth. New York: Brunner/Mazel, pp. 163-184.

Wolff, P. (1959), Observations on Newborn Infants. *Psychosom. Med.,* 21:110-118.

———— (1960), The Developmental Psychologies of Jean Piaget and Psychoanalysis. *Psychol. Issues,* Monogr. No. 5. New York: International Universities Press.

———— (1963), The Early Development of Smiling. In: *Determinants of Infant Behaviour,* ed. B. M. Foss, 2:113-134. New York: Wiley.

———— (1966), The Causes, Controls, and Organization of Behavior in the Neonate. *Psychol. Issues,* Monogr. No. 17. New York: International Universities Press.

———— (1967), Cognitive Considerations for a Psychoanalytic Theory of Language Acquisition. In: Motives and Thought: Psychoanalytic Essays in Honor of David Rapaport, ed. R. Holt. *Psychol. Issues,* Monogr No. 18/19:300-343. New York: International Universities Press.

Yarrow, L. (1967), The Development of Focused Relationships during Infancy. In: *Exceptional Infant,* Vol. 1. *The Normal Infant,* ed. J. Hellmuth. New York: Brunner/Mazel, pp. 427-443.

————, Klein, R. P., Lomonaco, S., & Morgan, G. A. (1975), Cognitive and Motivational Development in Early Childhood. In: *Exceptional Infant,* Vol. 3. *Assessment and Intervention,* ed. B. Z. Friedlander, G. M. Sterritt, & G. Kirk. New York: Brunner/Mazel, pp. 491-502.

Zelazo, P. (1972), Smiling and Vocalizing: A Cognitive Emphasis. *Merrill-Palmer Quart.,* 18:349-365.

———— & Komer, J. (1971), Infant Smiling to Nonsocial Stimuli and the Recognition Hypothesis. *Child Develop.,* 42:1327-1339.

INDEX

ABOUT THE AUTHORS

Robert Newcomb Emde received his M.D. from Columbia University, College of Physicians and Surgeons, in 1960. After a medical internship at the University of Minnesota, he completed his psychiatric residency at the University of Colorado Medical School and then served as head of the Western Division of Colorado State Hospital. Since 1965, he has been on the faculty of the University of Colorado Medical School where he is now Professor of Psychiatry and holds a Research Scientist Development Award from the National Institute of Mental Health. He completed his psychoanalytic training at the Denver Institute for Psychoanalysis in 1974 and is now a member of its faculty. He is also a member of the graduate faculties in Developmental Psychology at both the University of Denver and the University of Colorado at Boulder. He has served as Executive Secretary for the Association for the Psychophysiological Study of Sleep, on the Editorial Board of the *Journal of the American Psychoanalytic Association,* and as a member of the Commissions on Psychoanalytic Education and Research.

Theodore J. Gaensbauer received his M.D. from the University of Michigan Medical School in 1968. After an internship at the University of Southern California Los Angeles County Medical Center, he completed a residency in Psychiatry at the University of Colorado Medical School. He also held a Research Fellowship in Developmental Psychobiology in the Department of Psychiatry, and later served on active duty in the Air Force. He is now Assistant Professor of Psychiatry at the University of Colorado Medical School and a candidate at the Denver Institute for Psychoanalysis.

ROBERT J. HARMON received his M.D. from the University of Colorado School of Medicine in 1971. In the same year, he also received the Joseph and Regina Glaser Award for the most outstanding research by a medical student. Following two years of Residency in Psychiatry at the University of Colorado Medical School, he became a Research Associate at the Social and Behavioral Sciences Branch of the National Institute of Child Health and Human Development, where he has carried out a number of studies in the laboratory of Dr. Leon Yarrow. He is also a Clinical Instructor in Psychiatry and Behavioral Science at the George Washington University School of Medicine.

PSYCHOLOGICAL ISSUES